American Sign Language for Beginners

- 3 In 1 -

From Beginner to Fluency, Your Bible to Unveil the Beauty of Visual Communication in 21 Days. With Clear and Large Pictures

MARTIN BARLOW

Table of Contents

I hope you enjoy the book! If you find any errors or want to provide feedback, please write to mbagencypress@gmail.com. Thank you

Book1: ASL Basics: Mastering the Fundamentals

Chapter 1: Introduction to American Sign Language

American Sign Language (ASL) is a natural mode of communication, just like any other language. But, it is meant specifically to interact with people using hand gestures and facial expressions. For you to better understand ASL, you must know it is a visual-gestural language used mostly by the deaf community in both Canada and the United States. It is different from that of the spoken English and other such languages.

ASL is a full-fledged language with all of the associated properties, similar to that of any other spoken language. The only difference is that ASL has been developed and practiced independently and very differently from the English language. The grammar for ASL varies immensely from that of English and other languages. The North Americans who have hearing deficiency and are unable to speak, often prefer using this language to communicate with the friends and family members.

The people who are fit and fine must also learn this language in order to communicate with the members of their family who are physically challenged with hearing and speaking issues. ASL is specifically derived from the Americans for the Americans. But, in some or many other countries, people prefer using ASL as the primary approach to communication with such challenged individuals.

It is mostly because the ASL is quite sophisticated with clear illustrations on how hand gestures and facial expressions can easily convey the desired message that a person wants the others to understand. Even though a lot of countries prefer ASL, you must know that there is no universal standardisation on sign language. Every country has the liberty to prepare and use their own sign languages. For instance, the British Sign Language (BSL) is quite different from that of the ASL.

Hence, the people who know ASL, might not be able to understand BSL, and vice versa. There's no special committee who took charge on making ASL, and there are no evidences on how did it exactly start. But, some of the people suggest that, ASL is a 200 years old language, that has been taken from the local sign languages being used back then, which was an intermix with French Sign Language. The local term to describe that version of sign language is, *Langue des Signes Francaise (LSF)*.

You can conclude that today's ASL has some resemblance with that of the LSF, alongside the actual local signs of that time. Over the course of time, these sign languages and the lessons that were used by kids or adults to master them, were changed and amended. The LSF was converted into rich, mature and more complex language. Thus, ASL was born, and it is completely different from that of the LSF. But, you will find some similar signs, which isn't much in use in the modern days.

The formal education system accepted the need for helping the deaf kids receive academic qualifications, in 1817. There was an establishment of the American School for the Deaf, which was located in Connecticut. The mode of providing education in that school was through signs. And, it was the attempt for representing a set of syntax and structure of English, through the hand gestures and facial expressions. There was a positive hope, if the deaf students were given accessibility to the English structure, then they could possibly acquire it.

By adopting the visual form of conveying the English language, the deaf students were then able to attain their academic achievement, with the writing and reading skills in hand. The early version of Signed English was relying upon the Signed French language. It is because the American instructions were mostly or wholly borrowed from the French model.

And in 1835, the ASL was primarily introduced in the schools for deaf students in America. Signed English was removed from the curriculum, as it was no longer considered the natural deaf language. Apart from that, the articulation and speech obtained through it wasn't emphasising much on the English language.

The use of ASL in the education curriculum of the deaf and dumb students has now been characterised as controversy and conflict. But, the people of America believe the challenged individuals need their own language to be able to be part of the normal population without feeling left out or side-tracked. Apart from that, the educational institutions in America is now also encouraging to add ASL as the mandatory subject in schools for all students, even for the ones who don't have any physical challenges in hearing or speaking.

It is because, for physically challenged individuals to be able to use ASL for living a normal life, it is important the people around them understand that language and would be able to communicate with them feasibly. And such initiatives by the educational institutions of United States, will definitely be a stand-out implementation.

In this book, we will be discussing on how you can master the fundamentals of ASL. The chapters ahead will discuss on all core considerations on ASL and its learning pattern. Every essential aspect that you must consider while learning ASL is well-elaborated in this book. You can then pass your learnings on as a knowledge to someone who is in need of it, or to be able to communicate with friends or family members who are physically challenged.

Chapter 2: ASL Alphabet and Numbers

Just like the usual English language, ASL also has a standard 26 alphabets and 10 numbers, for the students to learn and master their lessons from scratch. ASL doesn't recommend any absurd teaching process, and believes in starting the education from scratch. Just like the alphabets, the ASL also consists of distinct sign languages for representing the numerical quantities.

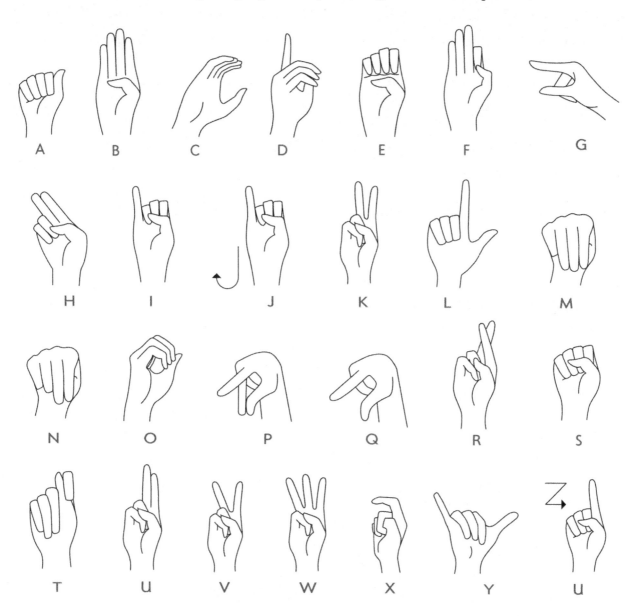

To help you understand how ASL excels in helping the deaf and dumb students learn better with numbers and alphabets, here's a brief explanation on all of them:

1. **A-** A is represented in ASL by a closed fist, where the palm will always be facing in the forward direction, irrespective of wherever it might be noted.

2. B- B is represented in ASL by a open palm facing front, where the thumb will be touching the base of the ring finger.

3. C- Palm should be facing forward, whereas the thumb should be bent out in order to form a C in ASL.

4. D- The palm will stay partially open, where the little, ring and middle finger will be bent to touch the thumb, while the index finger will be pointed towards the top, which forms a D.

5. E- To form an E, the thumb is often lowered, and the other fingers also come down, to represent a claw.

6 F- To form a F, the thumb and index finger will be bent to touch one another, while the palm and rest of the fingers stays open.

7 . G- To make the letter G, you need to make a fist and then extend your index finger and rest your thumb against your middle finger. Your palm should be facing you and the index finger should be pointing to your left.

8. H- Stick out your middle and index fingers outwards while keeping the same fisted position as you did for G. The palm should be facing you and the fingers should be directed to the left.

9. I- Making the I with your finger is done by sticking out the pinkie while all other fingers are fisted. This makes the sign of I.

10. J- From the pinkie position of I, you can then bring down the single finger in a manner to show the shape of J. First bring down the finger and then scoop it upwards to make J.

11. K- Point the index and middle fingers a little apart from each other and the thumb between them. The two fingers should make a victory sign with thumb between them. The palm should be facing away from your body.

12. L- At first, fist your hand and raise it up, then open up your thumb and your index finger to show the shape of L.

13. M- Fist your hand like you are holding an imaginary ball. Then you need to poke your thumb through the ball and face the palm away from your body.

14. N- Make an invisible ball and raise your index and middle finger to an extent while keeping the knuckles bent to an extent. Then poke the thumb under the two fingers to support the two. The palm should face away from the body.

15. O- Press the tips of your fingers and thumb to make an O like shape.

16. P- Make a fist and bend it downward. Then you need to press your thumb against your middle finger. The index finger should be pointed to make the P shape. Extend the middle finger so that it points downwards.

17. Q- make the sign for the G letter and then point it downwards to create the shape of Q. Press your middle, pinkie and thumb finger into your palm . Point with the index finger.

18. R- Make a fist and raise your arm. Then extend the middle and index fingers. After this, cross the two fingers so that the palm is facing outwards.

19. S- Make your fist and then put the thumb on top of all other fingers to show the letter S.

20. T- Form a fist from your upright dominant hand. Then put the thumb between the index and middle finger sot that the thumb nail is visible partially.

21. U- Make a fist and align it upright position. Then extend the middle and index fingers in a way that the two fingers are joined and point towards the same direction.

22. V- Make the same sign as U and then spread the index and middle fingers apart to make a V like shape.

23. W- Raise the arm and hold up three fingers of the middle, index and ring one. Then spread the three fingers so that there is distance and there is a shape of W.

24. X- Make a fist and raise the fist with the arm. Then point out the index finger and crook it to create a partial hook.

25. Y- The Y letter can be done by fisting the dominant hand. Then you need to stick out the pinkie and the thumb so that there is a y like shape.

26. Z- To make the sign of Z, raise your hand in a fist and then take out your index finger. After this, make the pattern of Z for the sign of Z.

ASL Numbers

Signing numbers is very easy if you know which fingers to use and the transitions between different numbers. You have to remember the order in which the numbers go in sign.

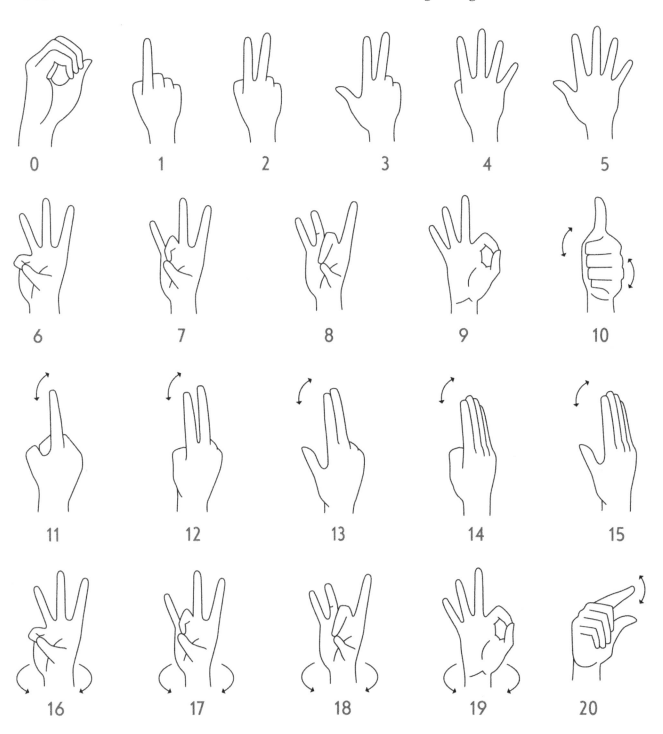

For 1-5

For 1-5, your index finger is raised first and then index and middle for 2, index, middle and thumb for three. All but thumb fingers are raised for four and all five fingers are raised for five.

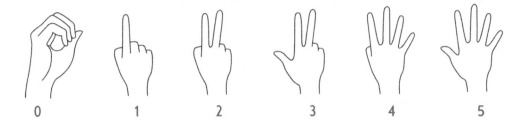

For 6-10

The number for 6 to 10 can be signed using the one hand too. The numbers are signed by touching a finger to the thumb. The fingers are extended outward. Then, you need to touch pinkie to thumb for 6, ring finger to thumb for 7, and middle finger to thumb for 8. You also touch index to thumb for 9. The number 10 is shown by creating an A and shaking the fist with thumb up.

11-15

To sign the numbers 11 to 15, you need to flick your fingers up two times, palm back. To show the sign of 11, you flick your index finger up two times. For 12, the two middle and index fingers are flicked together. For 13 you sign in a thumb out and two fingers pressed together, bending in rather than flicking out.

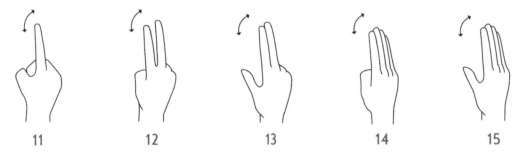

For 14 and 15 it is also bending in but for four fingers and five fingers respectively.

For numbers 16 to 19, the higher number is the base number twisted twice in a palm back manner. 16 is 6 number twisted twice, 17 is 7 twisted twice and so on. For 20, you need to tap the thumb and index finger together twice. Other fingers should be bent at the knuckles to face the palm inwardly.

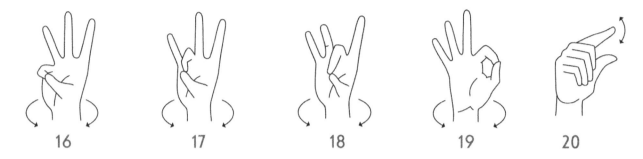

To sign other decade numbers, you need to sign out the first number on its own and then sign out the sign for zero. For example 30 is signed by signing the sign for 3 and then zero. This can also be done for 40, 50, and so on.

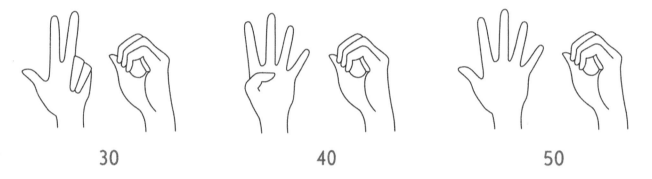

These are the basic numbers you need to know the signs of in the beginners' phase.

Chapter 3- Basic ASL Vocabulary

To start talking in ASL, you need to know the basic ASL signs so that you can use these in daily conversations. In this chapter, you will learn about the basic words that can be signed with ASL gestures.

Boy

To do the boy sign, you need to grab the brim of an imaginary cap sticking out of your forehead and open and close your hand.

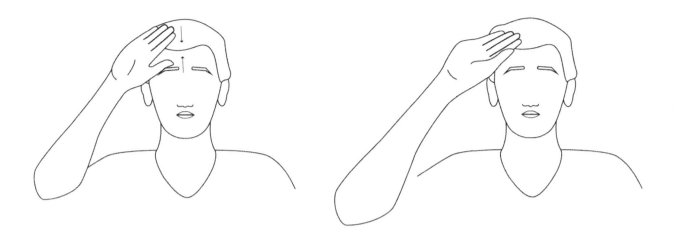

Girl

For the girl sign, make an A with your hand and bring it to your cheek. After this, trace along your jawbone and line it with the tip of your thumb.

Adult

To sign an adult or to show that someone is a grown up, you need to put your hand with your fingers outstretched but together and the thumb tucked. You then have to keep this hand at shoulder level or just below your chin. After this, you need to move this hand slowly to your head level.

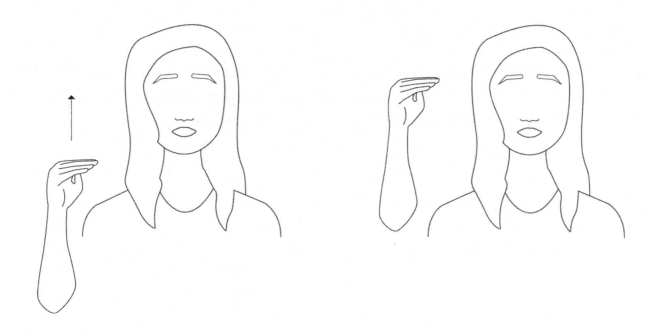

All

To sign all, you need to open both your hands with one palm facing you and the other not facing you. You then make a sweeping, circular hovering motion with your right hand around your left hand. After this circular motion, let the hand rest on the right hand in crossed manner and close to your chest.

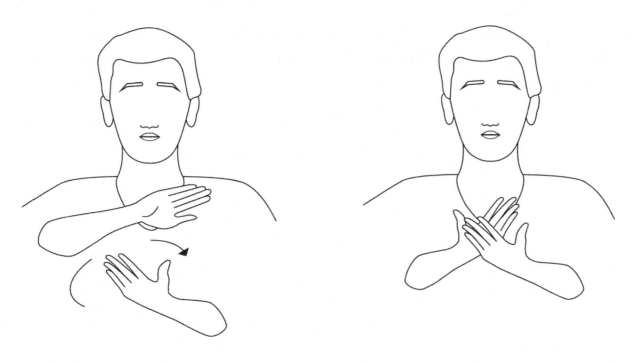

Back

To make the back sign, you need to raise your right arm like a fist and take out the thumb to point at the ceiling. Then you need to move it in such a manner that the thumb rests over your shoulder and points to your back side. You can move it back and forth to put emphasis.

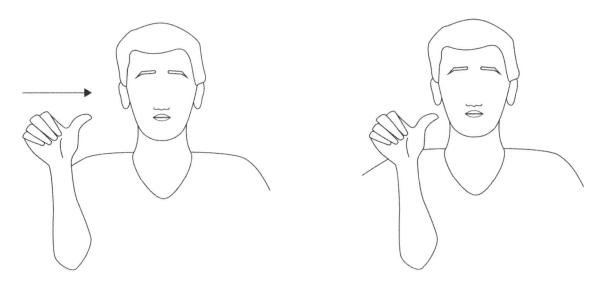

Bad

Bad is a generic adjective that can be used in many context. To show the action for Bad, you can touch your chin with your right hand with only the fingertips. Then, you can move your hand away from the chin, flipping it to expose the open palm. When doing this, make a serious face to put emphasis.

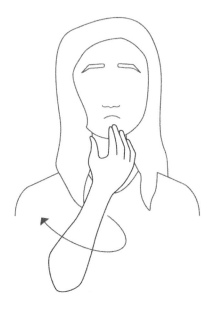

Call

To make the sign for call, you need to point out the pinkie and the thumb to make a y shape. Then bring the hand near your head and ears with your pinkie touching your chin. Then move the hand forward a little bit to show the calling action.

Cake

To sign for cake, place the left hand at your stomach level with your hand flat and facing upward. The left hand acts like the base of a cake. After this, you can put your right hand on top of the left hand in a upside down cup shape and then raise it upwards to show a cake.

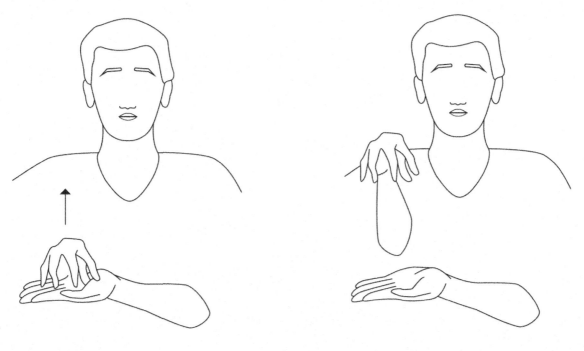

Car

To show the sign of a car, make a sign like you are holding an imaginary steering wheel. Then start moving it round and round to show the movement of a car and the act of driving.

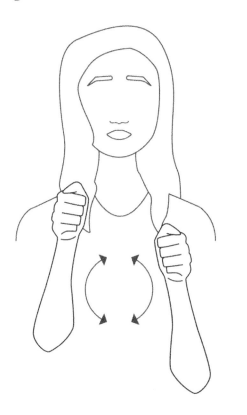 

Name

Eat

Breakfast

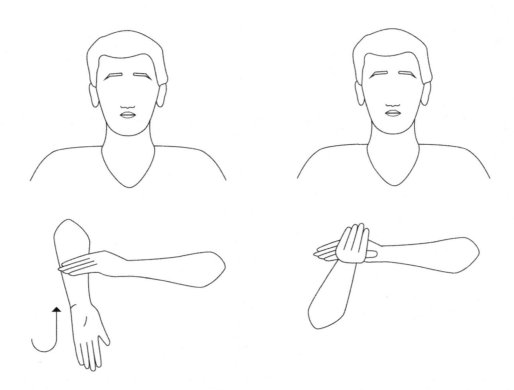

19

Bed

Toy

Water

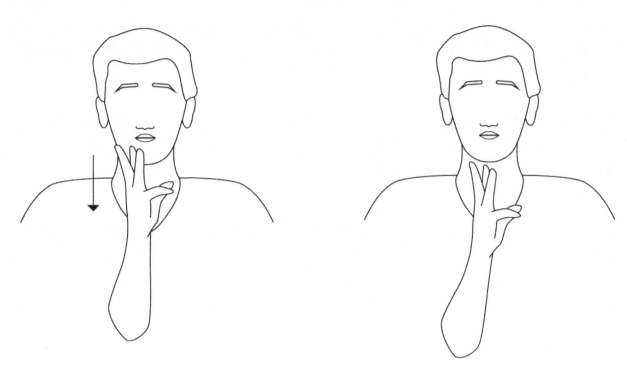

All done

These are some of the basic words that you should learn to talk and point at common objects.

Chapter 4- Sentence Structure in ASL

ASL follows the grammatical rules, just like the sentence structuring of the American English. In case of ASL, it is bit different, as the structuring goes in an order, which represents, *subject+verb+object.*

ASL doesn't consist of any kind of verb conjugations for its several verbs. But instead, it combines the signs of several words for indicating the tenses. To help you understand, here's a proper example. Suppose you say "I am hungry" in English. In that case, the ASL translation of the same sentence would be, "Me am hungry".

Now, you would definitely get the point on how sentence structure varies in ASL from that of the usual American English. As there aren't any verb conjugations within the ASL, the entire sentence structure gets affected. But, it is enough for the people to understand the language and take the communication further.

The ASL speakers also tend to communicate the verb tense through their hand placement and body movement. When the hand signs are performed closer to body, it indicates present tense. But, when discussing future tense, the hand signs performed farther from body, is a reference to the future. Hence, this sentence structuring and conveying nuances with the use of hand position and body language is considered remarkable.

Asl uses different sign orders to show a particular thing and make a sentence that is understandable. Which sign order is perfect for which expression depends on the topic and the context of the sign. The syntax and grammar also depends on what you are trying to explain and what you are trying to convey with the order.

Much like English, the ASL also has multiple signs that stand for one word. Depending on the context in which the word is used, the sign is different. For example, the sign for fear and afraid can be different or the sign sequence for can will be different as an object and as a verb.

The ASL grammar also does not use state of being verbs like be, were, was, is, are because it would complicate the expression. Instead of that, there are signs for the verbs and depending on the order, the person decodes the sentence.

There are many sentences that can be expressed in the topic comment format. For example, the topic is what you are talking about and the comments are the observations made about the topic. The topic is mentioned first and then the comments are mentioned through ASL.

Like if we say Boy Throw Ball, we are intending to say he threw the ball or the boy threw the ball.

Boy

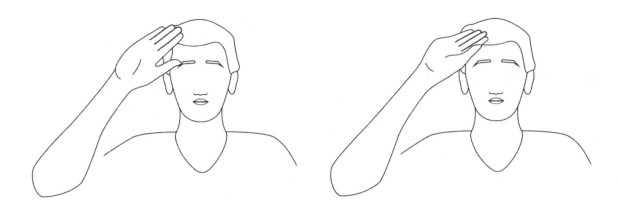

Throw Away

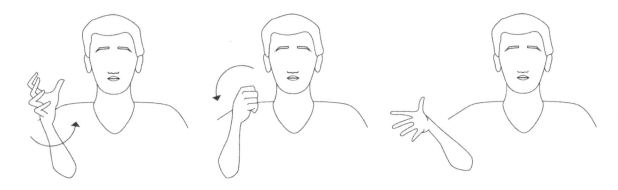

Ball

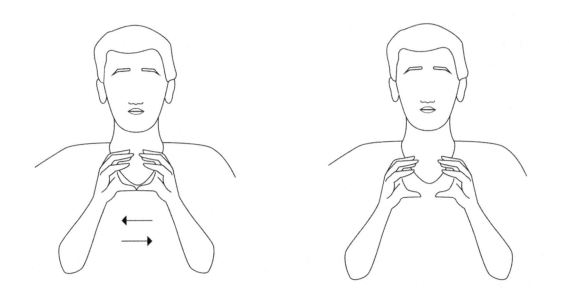

If we have to express the sentence I went to Ireland a year ago, then we would use a combination of Last year me (go +finish) Ireland. The ASL grammar simplifies the verbs and conjugates them so that the sense is delivered. We string together words through signs and make sentences to deliver the meaning.

Chapter 5- Asking Questions in ASL

In this chapter, we will learn about the way to ask questions in ASL and creating conversation by asking questions. There are some question words and signs like question mark that are necessary for asking questions. When we use English, our question framing is different. In ASL, although we use the same words, the order and the signs differ. When you want to ask a question, you make a sentence or use the words indicating the noun and verb and then add a question word to the end of the sentence. After adding the question word, you also need to add the question mark sign manually through signs.

When you start asking questions, you can also make your facial expression in such a way that it shows your inquisitive ness and your curiosity. As you sign the question mark, lean a little forward, and look inquisitive. To show your inquisitive ness you can scrunch up your eyebrows. You should then tilt your head to the side to show your questioning expression.

Who

With the right hand, place your thumb on your chin. Then you need to wiggle the index finger from the knuckle. The other three finger curl under your palm and touch the cheek.

What

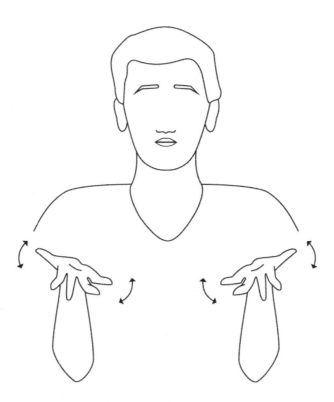

To create the sign for what, you need to put your hands outwards so that the hands are in front. The elbows should be bent up and the palms should be facing up. To show the sign for what, shake the hands back and forth towards each other.

Where

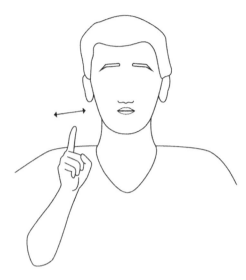

To make the question of where you need to hold up the index finger of your right hand. Then you need to shake the finger from side to side.

When

Point out the index fingers of the two hands and then place the two index fingers in such a way that there is a 90 degree angle between them. the right index finger should then make a circle around the standing left finger. After making a circle, the finger returns to its proper place.

To make the sign for which, you need to make both hands into fists. After making both hands into fists, point out the thumbs. Then make a up and down movement which makes an alternate movement between the two fists.

Which

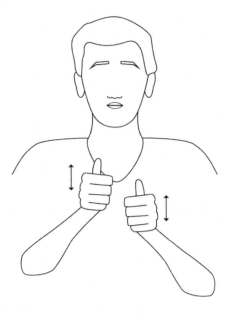

Why

You can make the why sign touch your forehead with the fingers of your right hand. Then, you can extend your thumb and pinky in a Y sign. After this, you need to bring your hand down. The middle fingers should be in and pointed towards the chest.

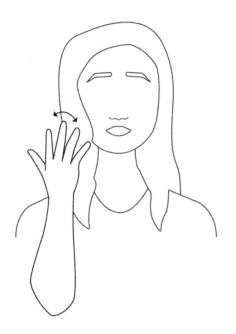 

How

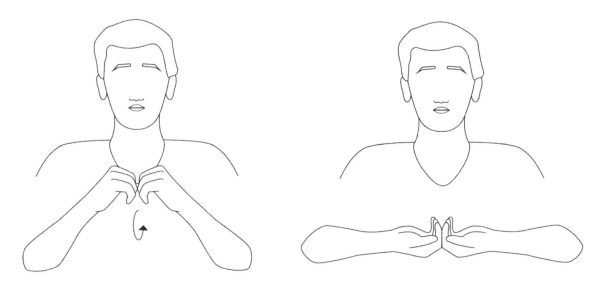

To make the sign for how, you need to point your finger downwards and your finger backs and the knuckles should be touching each other. Roll the hands inwards and towards your chest. Then take it up so that the pinky side of the hands are touching each other. These are the basic question words that you should be learning as basics of grammar for ASL sentences. When using these words, you have to maintain the right kind of facial expression too. There are some examples of simple questions below that you can ask in a very easy way with ASL.

Who is going?

To sign for the sentence of who is going, we can sign out going who followed by a question sign.

Another common question that we ask is **What do you mean?**

To sign for what do you mean, you can sign Mean, what and then the question mark. You is not usually signed because it is understood that the conversation is happening between two people and the person is asking the other person who is assumed you here.

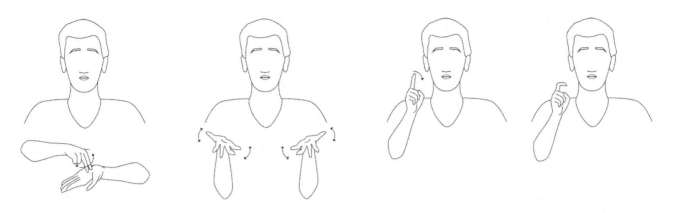

You should also know how to sign for ask so that it indicates a question or a prelude before asking a question. The sign for ask is done by pointing the index finger towards the person you are asking to and the hooking the index finger to create a question mark like sign.

Ask

There are also signs for request which can be used to ask a question politely. The sign for request is folded hands and then moving it up and down in the direction of the person you are requesting to.

Request

The above words are some of the most basic question and request words that you can sign with ASL. By using these signs and the facial expression you can successfully ask questions and start conversations.

Chapter 6- Expressing Emotions and Descriptions

When we make movements and signs to express sentences, we should not forget to express our feelings. The feeling and emotions we sign associate the sentence with descriptions. To make a sentence descriptive and connected with a situation, you need to use signs to indicate the emotions attached to them.

Here are the common emotions which you should sign with your fingers in ASL.

Angry

To make the angry sign, you need to open your palm and place the five fingers near your nose and eyes. The palm should be facing towards the face. Then you need to pull the hand away from the face while bending and scrunching up your fingers. In this sign, the scrunched-up fingers represent the furrows that appear on hour face when you are angry.

Happy

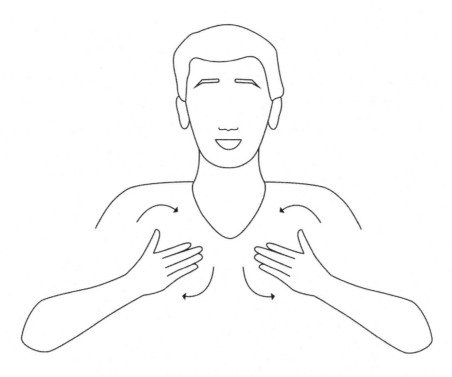

When signing the happy sign, you need to rotate one or both hands in front of your chest. The palm should be flat towards your chest and your thumb should face up while your hands are rotating. When you use one hand, it shows that you are happy. When both hands are used to express the emotion it shows overflowing happiness. So, depending on the degree of emotion, use this sign. You should always keep a smiling face when expressing the happy emotion.

Sad

Before you sign sad with your hands, you should use your face to express the emotion. For example, your lips should be pursed and drooping and your eyes should look sad. After this, you need to sign sad by dragging both your hands down your face. The hands do not have to touch your face, but the palms should be facing your face. The dragging of palms shows the track of tears to express sadness. The fingers should be spread wide, and the tracks should be traced from the eyes. Sadness can be shown with one hand, but it is always more impactful when you do it with both hands.

Worry

When you are worried, the emotion can be expressed as waving flat hands in front of you. These hands can be placed on either side of your head or by your ears. The palms should face each other. Use circular motion with each of the palms to show the worry emotion as a wave. The waving motion shows the waves and instability of anxiety and overthinking that we experience when we are very worried. The motion can be done in front of the face or the chest.

Sorry

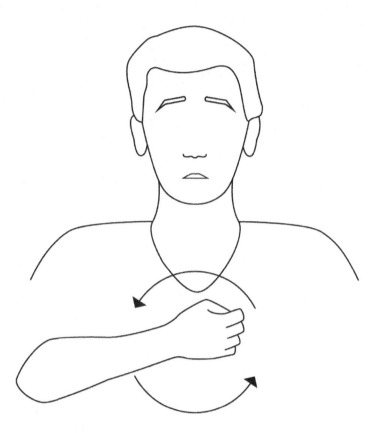

Suppose you are feeling sorry and want to express it. How will you express sorry in ASL? To express sorry, you need to make an apologetic face first. Place your fist, with the palm first direction over your heart and make a circular motion. the repetition of this movement, shows that you are really sorry and puts emphasis on the feeling.

These are the basic feelings and signs that you should use to express your emotions while signing for general sentences. Emotions are a crucial part of human conversations and every language, including ASL can express it easily. To sincerely express your emotions, make sure you are matching the movements with the facial expressions associated with the emotions.

Loving

Surprised

Lonely

Chapter 7- Time and Dates in ASL

Signing the date and time is an important part of passing information and holding conversations. When you want to tell the date and the time, you can make the signs associated with calendar, and the watch or clock and then sign numbers to indicate the right date and time.

Calendar

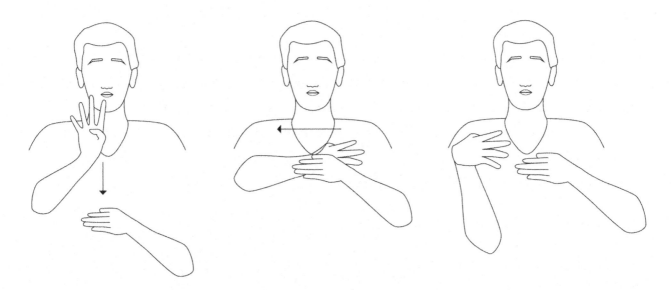

Telling the date

Date

To sign for the date, many people sign for the calendar followed by the letter linked with a certain month. For example, to show the date of January, the signer will use the sign for calendar and then sign J and then the date number. However, only signing J can be confusing because you are signing a letter that is linked with other months like June and July too. So, instead of signing for only the first letter of the month, you sign for the first three letters of the month. If you want to be more accurate, you can sign for all the letters of the month.

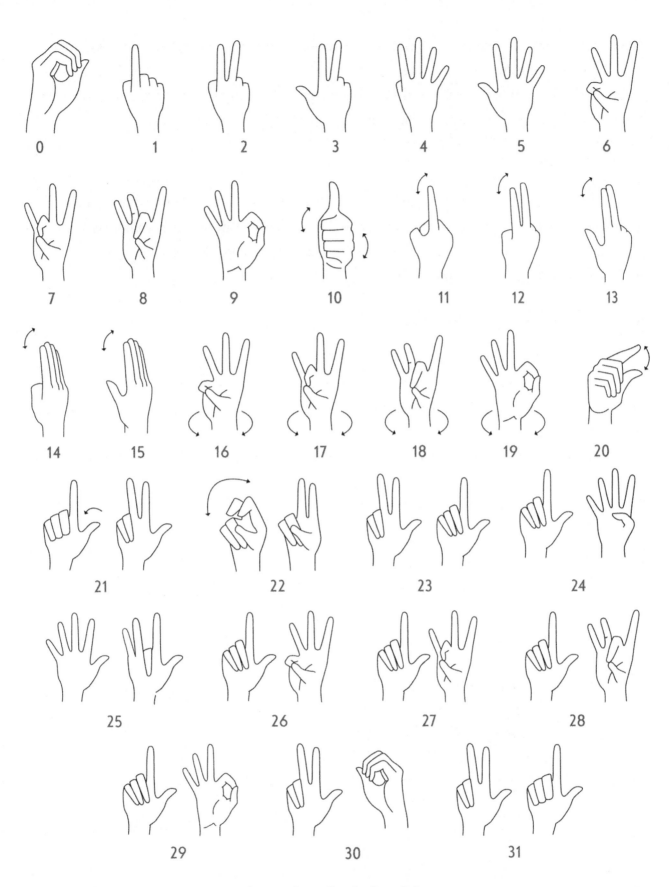

ASL numbers for clock and date

Then you can sign the number associated with the day and then sign out the number associated with the year. For example, if you are signing for 16 June 2023, you will sign JUN as individual letters and then sign for 1 and 6 and then after a gap of a minute, sign 2023 as number signs. Mostly March, April, June, July, May need to be properly spelt out in signs without abbreviation.

Telling the time

When you are going to sign time, always start from the surface of your wrist to denote the wristwatch or clock which stands for a measurement of time. Tap or touch your wrist with your finger and the off of your wrist make the number sign back to back. For example, you can sign for 4:30 by signing for 4 and then for 3 and 0.

Time

You can also use the flat of the raised left hand as the clock face. The index finger of the right hand can be used to show the second hand or the minute hand on the clock face. You can also circulate one hand around the clock face to show the passing of one hour or two or so on. To show the number of hours, you can circulate your right hand around the left clock hand as many times and then sign for the number on top of the clock hand.

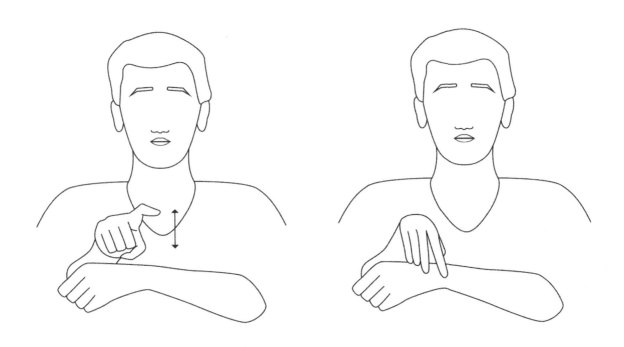

38

Book2: ASL Grammar: Building Blocks of Communication

Chapter 1- Verb Conjugation in ASL

Every language has its rules of grammar and ASL also has its own rules for tenses and time. The way we express tense and time in English, it has to be different in ASL because there are tautological limitations to the language and its expression. To speak fluently in ASL, you need to use your body and your hands. You need to know how to express English through hands and also work the tenses with the help of your hand signs. Before we show verbs and tenses with the help of our body, we see our body in the present tense. The time and tense that you show should be in sense of your body and come across very clearly.

Tenses and relative time

For present tense, the signing is pretty easy. When signing for present tense, you sign close to your body. Usually, most of the conversations in ASL happens in present tense and the person signs close to his body to show the present tense.

Past tense: AGO

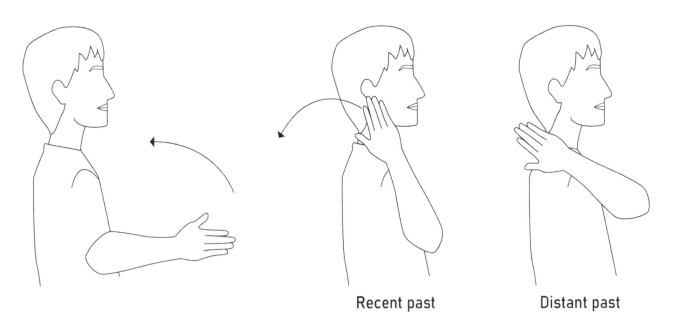

Recent past   Distant past

Present tense: NOW

Future tense: AGO

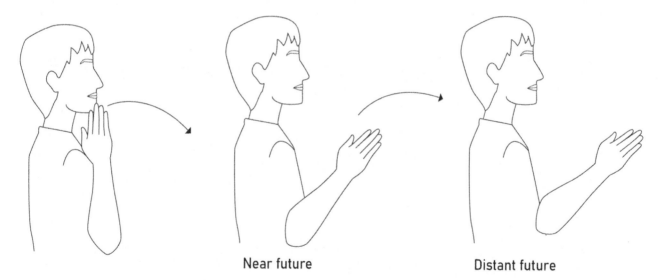

Near future   Distant future

However, signing in past tense can be a little difficult and takes some practice from beginners. To sign in past tense so that it is clear that the event you are speaking of took place in the past, you need to sign finish at the chest level to show that the action has already finished. The finish sign can be done at the beginning or at the end of the sentence when conveying. Most people who sign through ASL place the finish word at the beginning of the sentence to show past tense.

Finish

For the future tense you need to sign a different word at the beginning of the sentence. To show the future tense most people sign will at the end of the sentence. The farther you will sign, the word will from your body, the farther the prospects of future go. It means that if you are going to sign for something that will happen tomorrow, it should be closer to your body than something that will happen next week. The distance shows that something is closer to present than other. The easiest way of signing for future is to mention the action that is going to happen and then add will at the end of the sentence through sign.

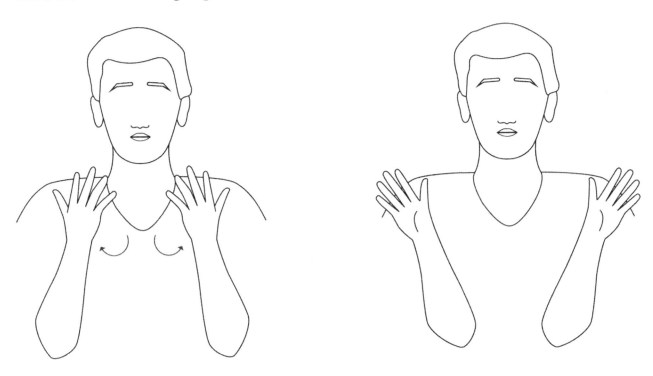

Will

There are different rules of using participle in ASL. In the ASL, the use of to is not done. Moreover, perfect tenses are also not signed for because these are passive tenses and can be very complicated to understand through sign. Therefore, in ASL, you only get to sign future, past and present tenses.

In ASL, you do not have the provision to sign verbs in ed or s or -ing form. By making the sign of now, you can show that the action is happening in present tense. The now word shows that the whole action is happening and is in continuous tense of present. For example, if you want to convey, I am going to the store, you can simply sign Go and then I followed by the sign for Store. Before you sign the sentence, you need to add the word Now in terms of signs.

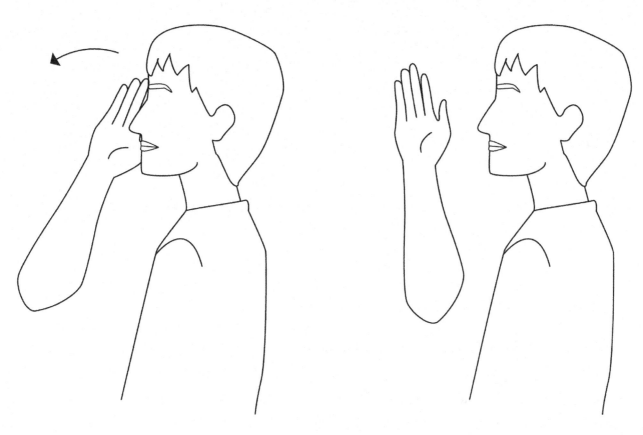

Store

By including the sign of Before in the sentence right before the actions can show past tense. For example, if you want to sign, I went to school, you need to sign Before at chest level and then sign for School and then I followed by Go. Instead of Before, you can also add Finish to the beginning or end of the sentences. Similarly, if you do not know how to sign for Will in ASL, you can sign for Next and add that word to the sentence at the beginning. This shows that you plan to do something next in the immediate future. If the sentence is I will go to school, you can sign Next, and then sign School followed by I and Go.

In the ASL, you need to substitute the to be verbs for interpretation. For example, in English, in the present tense we use is, are, am. However, you cannot sign these words in ASL. Instead, you sign now or present for these groups of words. On the other hand, will be is a word that we use in English. However, if you see, you cannot sign be in ASL. For that, you need to sign Will through your hands and the distance from your body.

Was and were are used in English to show past. However, you cannot sign for was and were in ASL. Instead, you need to sign for before or past or finish to show that the action has happened before the present time or is already finish. Although you cannot sign for be and to be, you can sign for become. You can sign for sentences like I become angry or I become sick with the help of ASL. Once you practice the relative distance from body and the phrases linked with past and future, you can sign for different tenses easily through ASL. With practice the speed and clarity of signing comes through.

Chapter 2-Pronouns and Possession in ASL

Possessive and pronouns are most commonly used in sentences. It is very easy to express the possessive sense and pronouns in English. However, to express possessive and pronoun through ASL can take learning new signs and movements so that they are clear to the viewer. In the ASL, the pronouns like me, she, he, us, are shown by changing the handshape from an index finger to an open palm. The palm should be directed towards the person that is possessing the other thing. To show possessives, the palm is used in different ways. For example, to indicate mine, you place the palm b on your chest. To show his, you place palm b towards the person you indicate towards.

Examples

Hers also happens in the same way but for a female person. To show the sign for theirs, the palm b is used in sweeping motion to show that there are many people and the thing belongs to a group of people. If you wish to sign for general possession, you will need to sign the word have. To sign the word have, you need to place both the palms on the chest and your fingers should be straight and knuckles should be bent. Usually, we don't sign the apostrophe s to show possession. This is instead covered by signing in an order. The order of signing establishes the relationship of possession between the owner and the thing. For example, if your mother's dog is dead, you sign my mother dog dead. When you sign dog right after mother, it establishes the relationship without the need of an apostrophe s for possessives.

My

Mother

Dog

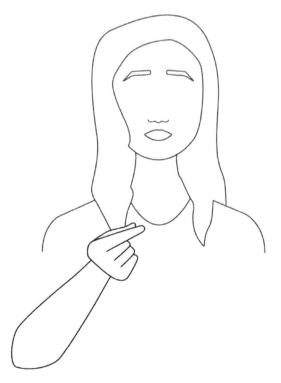

Dead

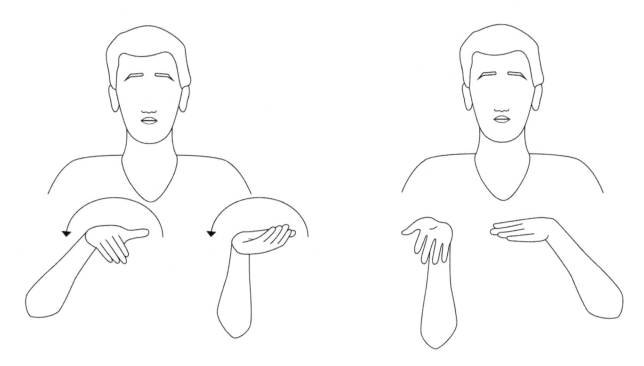

Common possessive pronouns

His, her and its is signed by the same gesture of the palm b signed outwards and the palm flat towards another person. For the sign of mine, you can sign by showing the palm on your chest in a flat manner. This can also be done for the pronoun my. The sign for our or ours is different. For this you cup your palm to create a c like shape. Then you place that palm on your chest. Usually this is done with the right hand placed on the left side of the chest. To show theirs or their, you can do a sweeping movement with the palm directed outward. However, you can sign the same in a different way by doing the his or her movement twice to reinforce the idea that there are more than one person to whom this thing belongs. You is signed by the open palm in an upright manner indicated towards the front of the other person in the conversation. If the word is yours and there are more than one person, then the same palm is held but the movement is a sweeping one to show that the thing belongs to you all.

His, hers, its, theirs

Our, ours

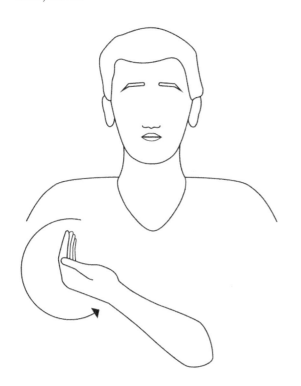 

Your or yours in sweeping movement

Basically, to use a pronoun or to show it is her, his, yours or theirs, you need to keep an open palm and indicate it towards the person or group of people it is directed towards. Instead of pronouns, you can also use the proper noun of anyone's name and then indicate that it belongs to him. for this, you need to finger spell the name of the person and then do the open palm gesture to show possession. This can also be done to ask about a thing and who it belongs to. For example, you can sign Matt and then point towards shoes or anything you want to know about and then sign a question mark.

If the sentence you are signing for is easy to sign, then it will not take many gestures. You can easily do the signs and sometimes the order of the thing and the pronoun does not matter. For example, you can sign My Dog and Dog Mine in the same manner and you do not have to change the signs too much.

Example

Therefore, use of possessive pronouns is possible in ASL grammar. However, there are no additional gestures as signs should be kept simple and easily understandable. For example, you can simply sign He is Rich by signing a gesture for rich and then signing the sign for him. For he has money, you can sign Money and then the gesture for him.

Money

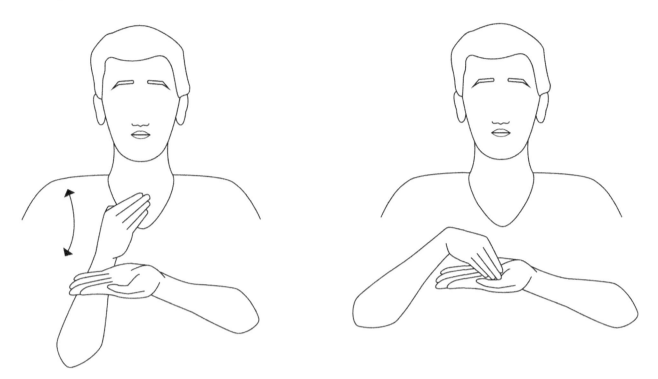

Him or her

There are many simple combinations that you can try to do for different possessive sentences. The main motto is to relay the meaning of the sentences to the person viewing the signs.

Chapter 3-Adjectives and Adverbs in ASL

In the English language, the adjective you use for a word usually comes before the word it describes. However, there are different rules in ASL. For example, if there is an adjective or adverb used, it comes after the noun or verb it describes. On other times, the adjective and the noun are expressed at the same time and this is clear by the hands expressing the noun and the face expressing the feeling or the adjective associated with the noun.

Ok

Most of the feelings and adjectives can be expressed with the help of your face and your expressions. You can move your facial muscles in such a way that the adjective is understood by the other party. For example, you can simply purse your lips and blow a little air while closing your eyes a little to show that something is small. On the other hand, you can puff out your cheeks to show that something is big. By shaping our eyebrows in a certain way or by moving our lips and cheeks in a certain way we convey a feeling.

Small

Tiny

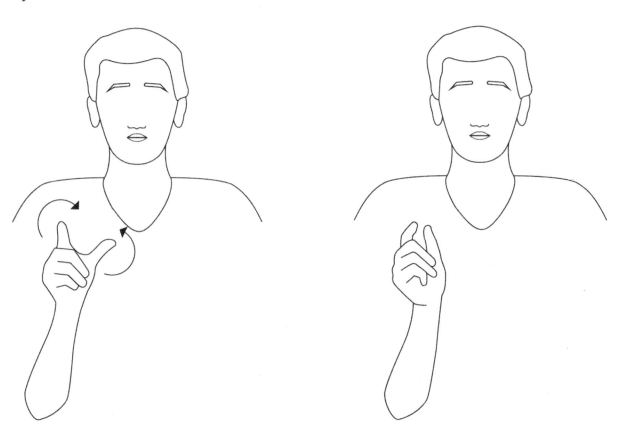

Big

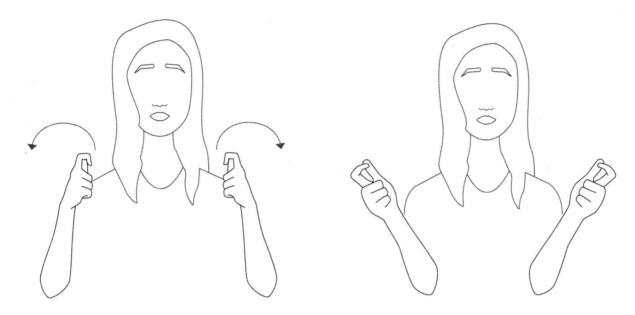

Signs for adverbs of time

There are some adjectives and adverbs that you cannot express in ASL. For example, very cannot be signed with ASL gestures. For adverb of time, there are some signs that can be repeated. For example, the sign for tomorrow can be repeated to show that something happens daily. One hand upright and a fist , is a sign for tomorrow. When this sign is repeated at different angles, it shows a daily occurrence. On the other hand, you can make the sign for week and then repeat it to show that it means weekly. You can also do the sign for month and then repeat it show that you are intending to say monthly.

Tomorrow

Day or repeated can be daily

Month and repeated monthly

Similarly, there are signs of day, night etc that can be done in a different manner to suggest that something happens all day or all night. When the day or the night sign is done in a bigger, longer movement, it shows that something happens for a long time and lasts for all day or lasts all night. You can also add a slight arching of the head to make the movement clearer and intention of description better. The sign for year is modified to show the yearly or annually sign. If you are suggesting days of the week and are talking about frequency of occurrence, you can do it with the help of downward sweep added to the sign for the day.

Year repeated yearly

Ugly

Particular words in adjectives have particular expressions. For example, there are so many adjectives that can be expressed. You can express the word ugly with the help of the index finger of a hand and placing that finger in a pointe direction under your nose. Then the finger is pulled in a straight line and then bent to show a hook.

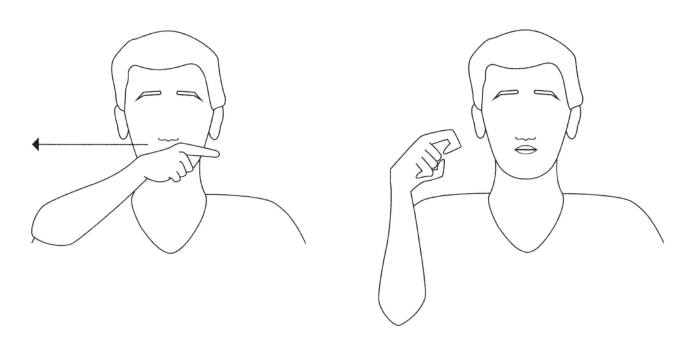

Short

On the other hand, to show the word short, you use your hand in a cupped way. You cup your palm and then raise that hand by your side to the head level. After this, you bring the palm down to your waist level to show that there is a decrease in height and the expression is short.

Ordinary

You can even express the word ordinary with the help of your hand. You bend your hand by the knuckles so that your fingers are folded against the inside of your palm. You then raise your hand and let the folded fingers brush against your cheek repeatedly. You should also purse your lips while doing this to show that the thing you are describing is an ordinary thing.

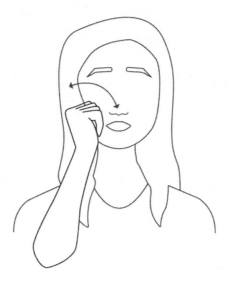

Regular

Suppose a deaf person has gone to a restaurant or a café where he has to order a regular coffee, he has to sign the word regular. Regular has a different way of signing as for this you need to cross your hands at your knuckles so that both the hands are juxtaposed with each other. The two hands can brush against each other too. After this, you need to take out your index fingers so that each of the fingers of the hand are pointing upward. Then you need to rotate the upper hand to show a round round motion for against the other hand.

57

Curly

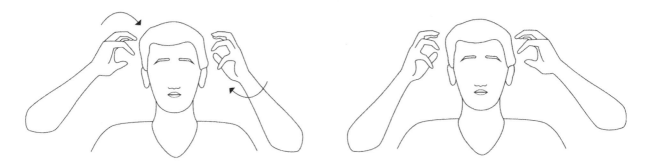

To show the word curly and intend that a particular thing is curly in nature, you need to sign each of the letters like C U R L Y separately so that the person can grasp the word and understand what is being signed.

Thick

You can also sign the word thick with your hands. For this, you need to place your palm parallel to the ground and at neck level. Your thumb and index fingers should be extended and slightly curled to show a curled L type of shape. Then you need to move your hand from the neck level upwards to mouth and nose level. The hand should not touch your face. Rather it should come up like bringing something up and in a forward motion.

Thick vertical

Thick

Medium or average

On the other hand, to show the word medium to show the level of a thing, you can use one hand in a horizontal manner and the other at a vertical direction, directed towards the palm that is horizontally aligned. Keep a palm horizontal and directed outward from your body. Raise the other hand and to chest level and direct it downward. As you bring that hand down on your other palm, rotate it as if you are mixing the air. The palm that is coming down should be put on the anchoring palm in a vertical and straight manner to show halfway or medium level.

Rude

There is a sign to show the rude word too. To sign that something or someone is rude, you need to raise your hand to chest level and cross two fingers the way we do to show a promise or when we interlock them. The fingers should be raised upwards. After this, the finger that is behind the other finger should be released and brought down by the knuckle. Then the whole palm should be folded to make a close fist. This shows that you are expressing the word rude with your hands.

Like this, there are many adjectives that can be expressed with the correct ASL gestures. Remembering so many adverbs and adjectives cannot be easy but with practice and proper attention to the movements it becomes very easy. You need to also see and learn the facial expression related to the movement so that the entire meaning is conveyed.

Chapter 4- Prepositions and Spatial Relationships in ASL

Like all other words in ASL, prepositions are also expressed with the help of signs and gestures. Prepositions like over, under, behind, are important to show so that a person can grasp the spatial relationship of a thing in a space. To deliver the sense of a sentence, expressing a preposition is important. For example, if you want to say books are on the table, omitting the on word during expression will take away the meaning of the sentence. Let us learn about the most basic prepositions and spatial words to show the position of something.

Over

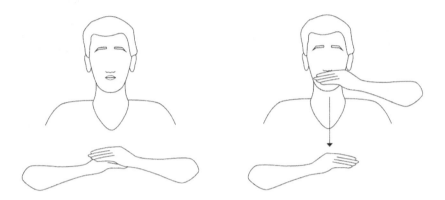

Over is a word that can be expressed with the help of your two hands. You need to place one hand in front of you and the palm directed downwards. Then you bring the other hand up and the palm directed the same way. You move the other hand on top of the one hand as if it is on the top of it but the hand should not touch the lower one. It should show that on thing is over another thing.

Under

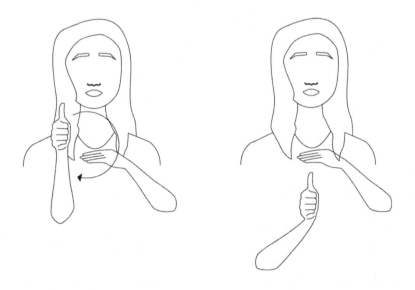

You can then show the sign for under with the help of ASL signs. For this, one hand should be flat by the palm and directed downwards. The other hand should be folded like a fist with the thumb out. The two hands should not touch each other and they should be placed without touching each other. At first the fisted hand should be on top of the flat hand. However, then to show the movement for under, you need to bring the fisted hand down, below the flat hand. The thumb of the fisted hand should be out and should slightly touch the flat hand palm. This shows the placement of one thing under another.

Next

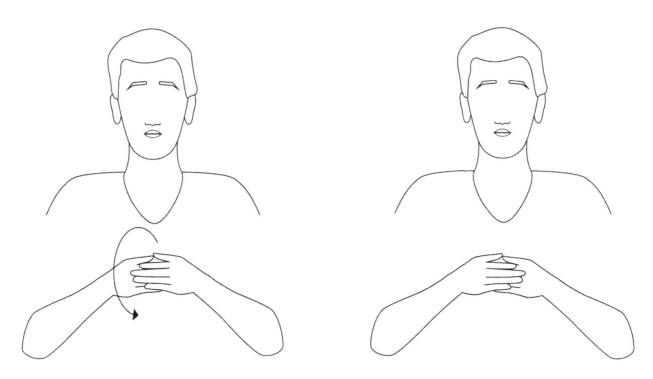

You can also show the word next to with the help of the hands in ASL. For this, you need to place one hand and the other hand, opposite to each other and the arms extended as if holding a box. One palm should face the other palm but the two hands should not be touching each other. In fact, there should be shoulder width distance between the two arms to show that one thing is next to the other but there is space between them.

In

You can also sign for the word in through the hand gestures of Asl. For example, you need to put one hand at chest level without touching the chest. The palm of this hand should be curled in a manner so that the knuckles should be facing outside and there is a hole in the middle that you can see from the top. The other hand or palm should be brought up so that it is above the other hand. The other palm should be bent slightly at the wrist and then brought down so that the hand is inside the hole of the other curled hand. This shows an inward motion and that one thing is inside the other.

In/Inside

 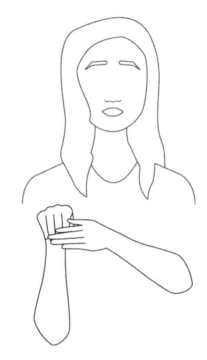

Front/ In front

The sign for in front of is very simple. This is a sign that is done from the head level to the chest level. The palm should be bent at the wrist so that it is in front of the head and the flat of the palm is directed towards the head. The palm should not touch the head. Then, once it is placed at the head level, you need to bring it down to the chest level so that the fingers are directed towards your chest. The arm should be bent away from the chest but the hand should be directed towards the person. This shows that the thing he or she is talking about is out at front and there is a distance between the two people or things.

Behind

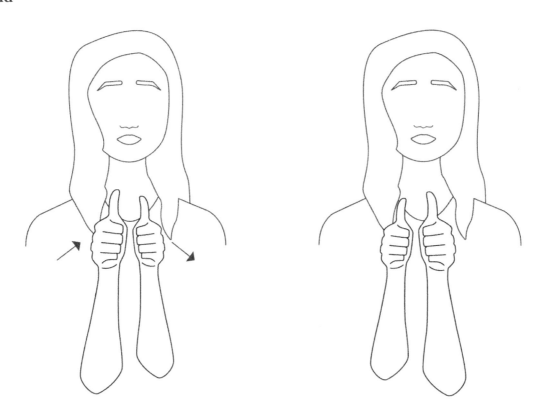

The gestures for behind should be done in a such a way that the two hands are at the same level but do not touch each other. The two hands should be at the chest level. The fingers of the two hands should be curled a little inward and only the two thumbs should be directed upwards. The two should be placed in such a way that one is slightly in front of the other. After this, you need to bring the front hand behind the other hand to show that one thing is placed behind the other. You can repeat this movement to show that one thing is behind the other in placement.

On

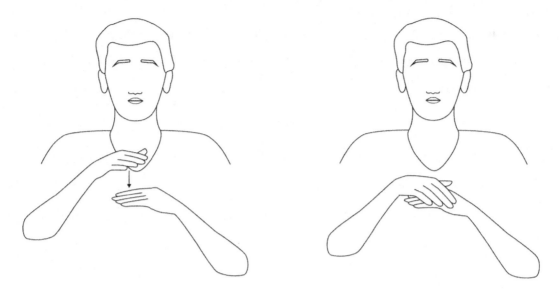

The gesture for on is a different kind of gesture where the arm and the hand are involved. This means that the arms are also in front of your chest. One hand is directed upwards and the forearm is upright. The raised hand is independent and in a vertical position as compared to the other hand. The two hands are not connected with each other. The other hand is bent in a horizontal manner at the stomach or chest level so that the forearm is in front of the stomach. The raised hand is then brought down so that one hand is on top of the other and the two forearms are placed in front of the chest. This means that one thing is on top of another thing.

Across

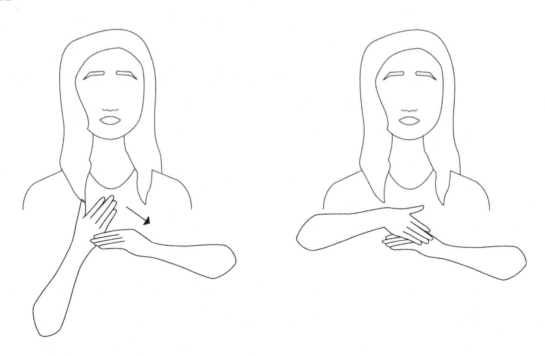

For the word across, you need to keep your both hands at the same chest level. One hand should be parallel to the ground and horizontal with the palm facing downward. Another hand should be behind the flat hand but it should be positioned in a vertical manner so that the side of the palm is touching the side of the horizontal palm. So, you create a cross like position with your hands to show that the position of the things is such.

After

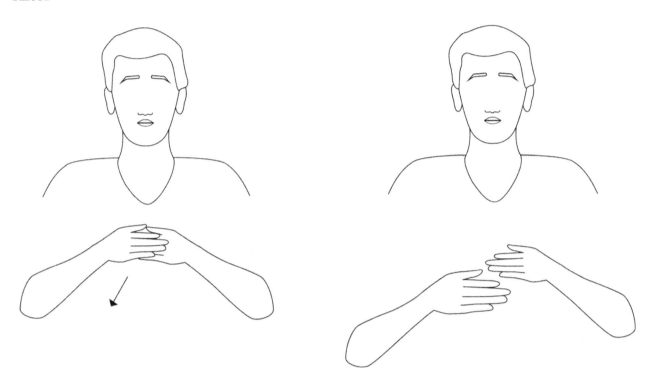

You can also sign after with the help of ASL language. For example, you need to do the same thing as you did in behind. The two palms should be flat and facing your body at chest level but not touching each other. The thumbs should be directed upwards. You should move one hand in such a way that it is in front of the other hand and it does not touch the other hand. The placement of one hand in front of the other shows that one thing is placed after the other.

Downward

For the downward movement, you need to put your hand by the side and your arm raised. The hand should be fisted with the thumb directed in the down direction. Then you need to move the fist in a downward direction from chest to waist level to show that the thing is moving in a downward direction. The opposite of this is done to show the upward direction.

Far

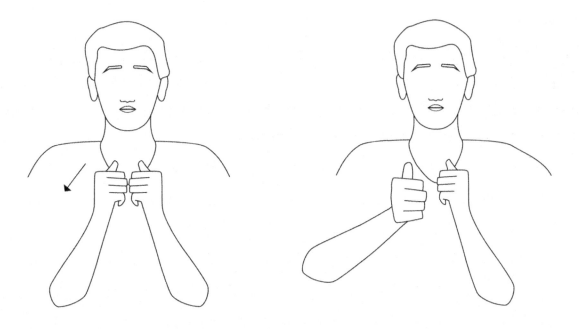

To show the movement for far, you need to curl up the two hands so that the fingers are facing inward for each palm. Then you need to touch the fingers of each hand together by the knuckles. The two hands should touch and be at chest level. After this, you need to move them apart in opposite directions and in a straight line to show that there is a considerable distance between the two.

These are some of the signs and movements that you can do to show spatial relationship between two things and to show a preposition. These signs are shown to indicate relationship between two things. Therefore, usually, both the hands are involved in establishing the relationship and show the relative position of each other. There are many other words like between, at that can be shown with the gestures of ASL.

Chapter 5- ASL Negation and Affirmation

Saying yes or no is a very common thing that everyone does when they communicate. The expression of negation and affirmations are very important and this can be done in ASL too. While in English we can negate and affirm with a simple yes or no, the signs of yes or no are a little elaborate in the tautological ASL language. In ASL, you need to move your hands to show yes or no. These signs should be learnt in a clear manner to convey the right kind of meaning in the sentence.

Affirmation/ Yes

For this, you need to keep your hands at chest level. At first, to say yes, you need to take a hand and make it into a fist. After making it into a fist, you need to move it back and forth. The bobbing motion that you will create in this manner shows the bobbing motion of the head to say yes. By doing this you can reply to something in an affirmative manner.

Negation / no

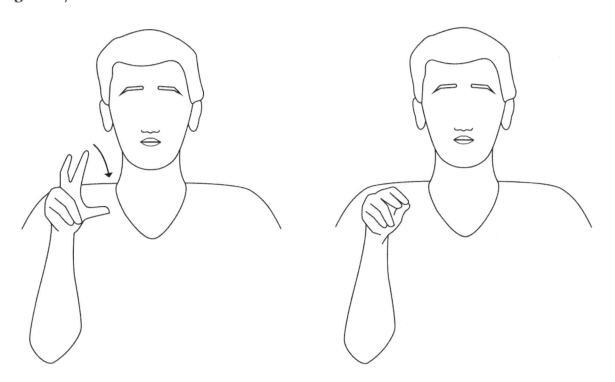

To say no, the motions are different. For the no motion, you need to show two of the first fingers and then tap the two fingers with the thumb so that it resembles a mouth saying no. While saying no or yes, you can also alter your facial expression to convey the emotion behind the gesture. For example, if it is a polite no, you have a pleasant or sorry expression. If it is a strong no and you feel quite opposite to what is being suggested, then your facial expressions will shift to those emotions. If you are happy saying yes, you can convey the emotion with the help of a smile.

Encouragement

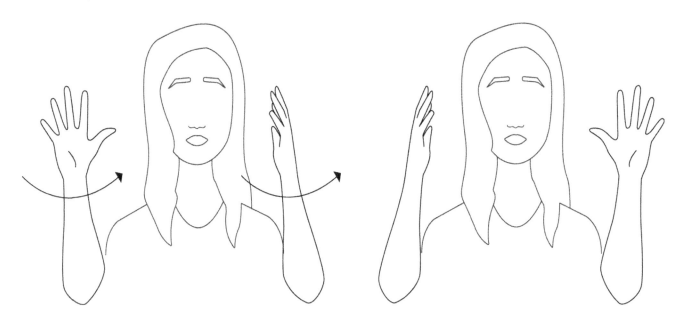

If you are doing a gesture to encourage and send affirmations their way like Hurray, or wow, you can raise both hands so that the arms are parallel to each other and the hands are directed upwards and then twist each wrist rapidly to show happiness and encouragement.

Not

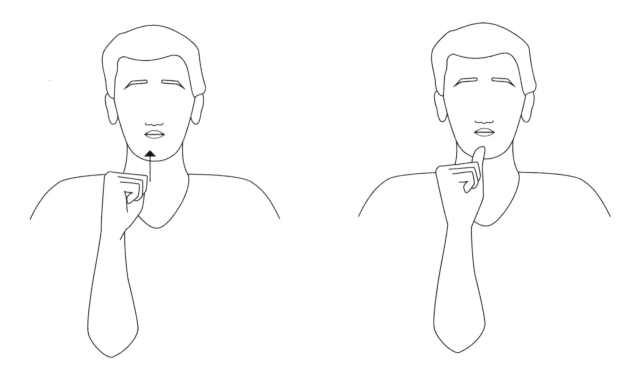

To sign the word not, you need to make a fist with your thumb out. Then you need to touch the thumb pad to your chin and shake your head in a negative manner to show the expression. While shaking your head, the fisted hand should move away from the chin and forward to a few inches.

Don't

You can also show the sign for don't with a simple crossing of flat hands at chest or stomach levels where the forearms are bent at elbow and horizontal. You then move the hands in their own direction to show the don't sign and also shake your head in a no.

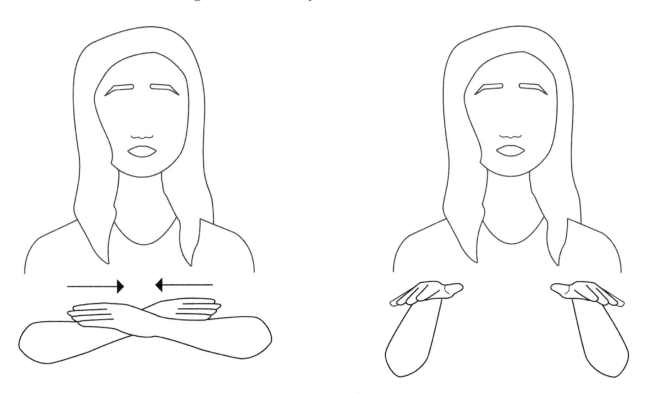

These are some of the signs that you can use to show affirmations and negations in ASL. These signs are pretty easy and can be used in daily conversations.

Chapter 6- ASL Classifiers and Descriptive Techniques

Descriptive classifiers are gestures that can be done in ASL to show the shape and size of a thing. The DCL gestures are somewhat like adjectives, but they are also very different from generic adjectives. The DCL is usually used to indicate a noun which is different from the gestures done for typical adjectives. One classifier can be used to describe a group or classification of things instead of one particular adjective.

Shapes and sizes

For example with a raised hand and your thumb and index finger curled to show a small hole, you can show the size of small things like buttons, eye pupils or a toy wheel and other small, round things.

To Show Round Objects Like Buttons

For a thicker or bigger comparison so that bigger objects can be classified, you need to use the same kind of formation but with a larger girth. If something is very big and thick, we can take our hands apart and motion like the two hands are holding and moving down a big, thick thing.

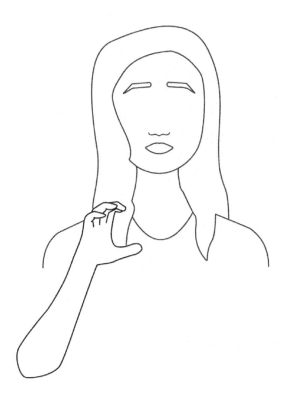

Classifier for thick vertical things like pipes

The orientation of the hands to classify can also change depending on the direction of the object. If the object is kept in a vertical manner, then the hands are aligned vertically, or they are aligned in a horizontal manner when the thing is placed in a horizontal manner.

Very thin and long objects in a vertical manner

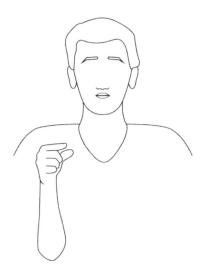

Associated with small movements like blinking and the movement of tweezers.

Different types of classifier words and gestures

There are different kind of classifiers in ASL. There are classifiers that show the appearance of the thing, then there are classifiers that show the location of the thing. There are plural classifiers and then there are body classifiers apart from shape and size specifiers. Depending on the noun you are classifying you use these DCLs. Body part classifiers are shown to show the movement of a body part in relation to a person or an animal. These are also used to show the location of the parts. In the body classifier group, the ASL instructor usually uses its entire body to show how the person moves to complete one action or how is the general behaviour of the person. Plural classifiers on the other hand show you the sign for different numbers.

Two people, plural classifier

The use of different classifiers in ASL brings variations and characteristic to the sentences.

74

Chapter 7- Expressing Time and Sequences in ASL

Asking about time or expressing time is a common behavior that we do in our day to day life. So, you need to know how to ask about time or express time in numbers with the help of ASL. The general expression of time is associated with the wrist because that is where you wear a wrist watch for the time. So, when you are asking about time, you can just tap or indicate towards your wrist top and then make the sign for question.

Wrist to ask time

Time/clock

On the other hand, when you are telling the time, you can simply do the wrist point movement and the taking away from the wrist gesture for the numbers in ASL. When this sequence is done one after the other, the time is conveyed.

You can also show the clock hand by raising a hand and facing the palm outward. Then you can use the other hand's finger to show the second hand, the minute hand or the hour hand. For the second hand, the index finger of the other hand moves once on the clock hand.

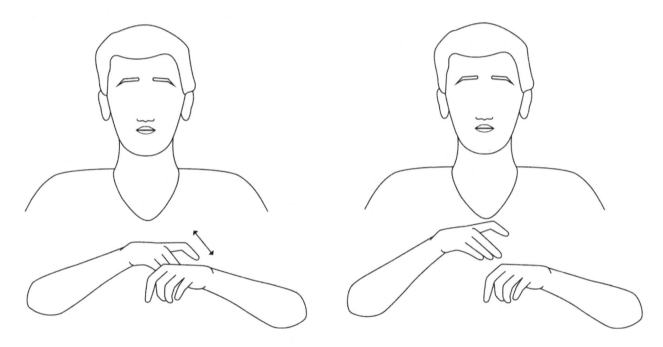

Minute

For the minute hand, the index finger moves twice and in a farther direction. For the expression of one hour we circle one hand in front of the clock hand to show the completion of one hour. After moving the hand in a round and clockwise manner, we can gesture for the number on top to show the passing of 2 hours, 3 hours, 4 hours and so on.

One hour

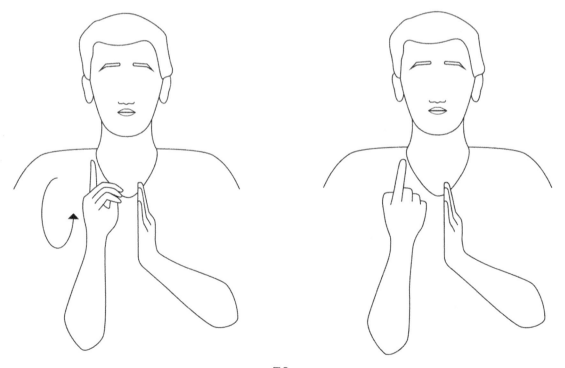

This can also be done for the minute or the second hand. For any number above nine, the number is expressed in a separate manner and then the hours or minutes are expressed at the clock hand.

Day

To show the time for one day, we use one hand in vertical and the other in horizontal placed close to one another. The index finger of the vertical hand is extended to show the position of the sun and time during the day. Then the vertical hand moves towards the horizontal hand till it is on top of it in a parallel manner. This movement shows the movement of the sun throughout the day to show the duration of a day.

Week

For a week, we need to hold out one hand flat, palm up to show you are holding a calendar. Then the other hand should have its index finger pointed out and then moved across the flat calendar hand to show the passing of a week. When you do this movement repeatedly, it shows the weekly routine.

Week and repeated weekly

Month

To show the month, you need to cross the two hands with the two index fingers pointed out. One hand should be vertically placed with index finger up and the other should be horizontally placed with the finger placed in a sideways manner. Then the sideways finger should move down the hand with the vertical index finger to show the passing of a month.

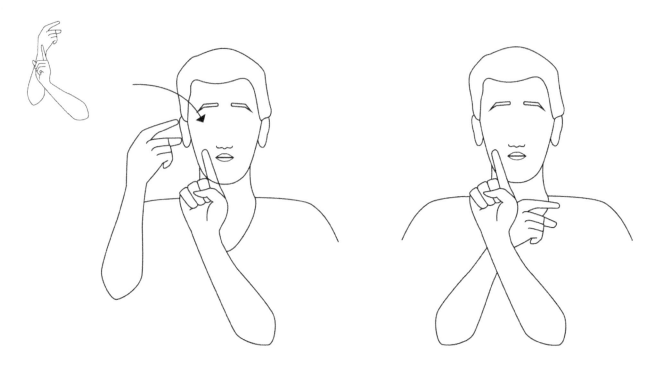

Month or monthly

Year

On the other hand, the word year can be shown by doing two fists and one fist moving around the other to show an annual cycle of the earth moving around the sun for one year.

Year and yearly

Sequences in a narration

Now that we know how to express time and routine, let us know how to express the sequence of things. To show the sequence of things in a narrative or conversation, you need to use different locations in your signing space to show the event sequence. Orient each location to the activity you are describing to show the specific position of that action in the sequence. Moreover, you can use your hands to gesture out Finish so that we know that one event or action has ended and the other event has started. You need to raise your brows and head at the beginning of the transitional activity and then lower your head to show the end of the activity.

Then

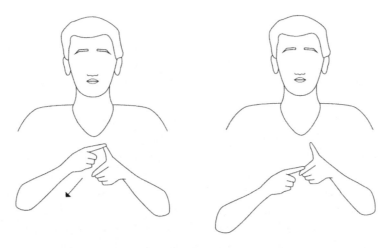

Book 3: ASL Conversations: Practical Communication Skills

Chapter 1- Greetings and Introductions in ASL

Greeting a person properly and giving introduction is an important part of any conversation. When you will be talking in ASL, even then you need to use greeting phrases and introductory words that help you initiate conversations. Even the basic greeting words and introduction style have expression in ASL. There are many words that you should learn if you want to start talking and having conversations in ASL. In this chapter, let us know about the words that can be shown with ASL gestures and signs.

Hello

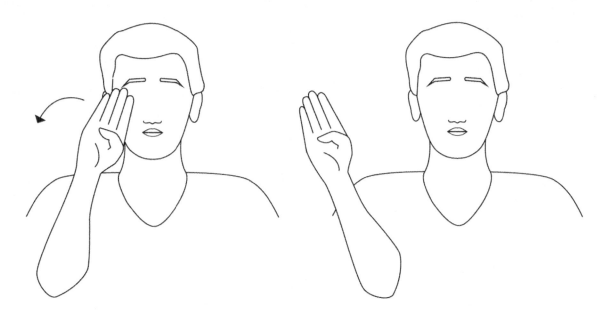

To gesture for hello, you need to start by putting your hand on your forehead. The fingers should be extended and the thumb should be touching your palm. After putting your hand on the forehead, you need to move your hand forward to show that you are saluting someone to say hello and show your respect.

What is your name?

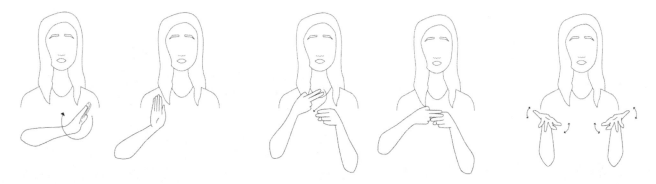

When you have to ask someone their name, you need to sign What is your name for them. Before starting a conversation with a stranger, you need to know their name. What is your name is a very common expression that can be a conversation opener. To ask what is your name, you need to place both the hands out in front of you. Your palms should be placed up. Shake the open palms and use a questioning expression on your face. Put your open right hand in front of you then bring the hand forward. Extend the index finger and the middle finger on both hands. Put right fingers on top of your left ones. Then tap the fingers twice.

My name is

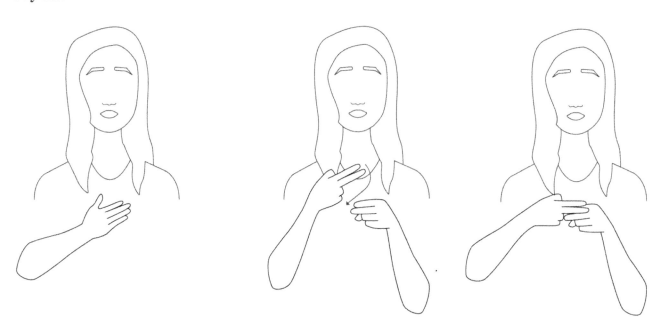

To answer the question of what is your name, you would need to sign the words my name is.. followed by your name. There are some signs and movements that you need to sign out for My name is... To say this in ASL, you need to place your right hand on your chest near your heart. After this, you need to extend the index and middle finger for both your hands. Put your right finger on top of your left fingers and then tap twice. After doing the sign for My name is, you can then sign your name using your fingers.

How are you?

As a pleasant way of starting a conversation, we use the expression of how are you for the other person of the conversation. You can say how are you using ASL. How are you can be expressed making two thumbs up and then holding them close to your chest. After this, you need to bring the two thumbs up down at the same time. Once you bring the thumbs down, ask the question by pointing the thumb towards the person you want to talk to.

I am fine

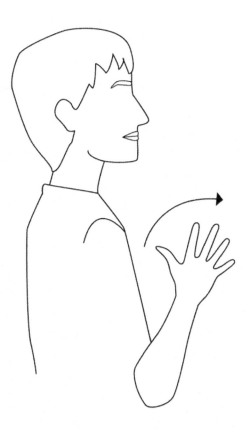

To the question of How are you, you need to say an answer of I am fine. By saying I am fine, you are politely continuing the conversation. To sign I am fine in ASL, you need to open your right hand and then rest it on your chest with your thumb touching your chest. Tap your chest with your thumb a few times to show that you are doing fine.

Thank you

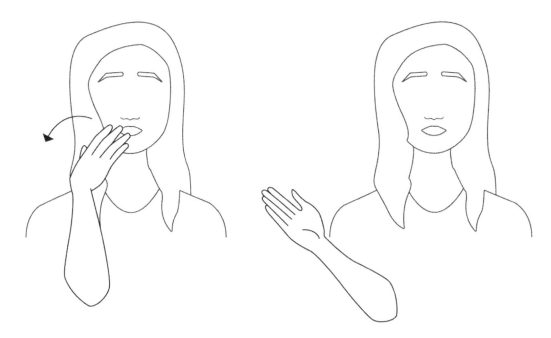

Thank you is a common polite word you need to say to express gratitude. You can use this word in your daily conversations when you are helped by someone or get a service from someone. To sign thank you, you need to flatten your hand so that your palm faces towards you. Then take the flat of the right palm upto your chin and then tap and extend this hand outward. This outward movement should be towards the person you are thanking.

Goodbye

You use the expression of Goodbye when ending a conversation or leaving a place. You can easily sign for goodbye using your hands. The sign for goodbye in ASL is an open right hand with the palm facing out. After this, you need to open and close your fingers as if you are waving goodbye to the person.

Nice to meet you

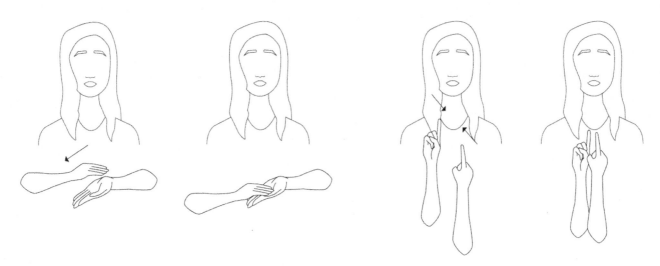

You can sign the expression of nice to meet you in order to show the other person that you enjoyed your brief meeting and the conversation you had. To sign meet you need to sign with two of your palms facing each other and brushing against each other. To sign for you, you need to point the index finger and the rest of the fingers should be tucked. The bump the two fists at knuckles to create a sign for two people meeting each other. To show the sign of you, you can point the index finger towards the person you are referring to.

Please

85

Please is a word that you need to sign to make a request and to talk politely. The word please comes in handy in multiple situations. You can do the ASL sign for please with the help of one hand. For this sign, you need to place the flat of your right hand on your chest. After placing the right hand on the center of the chest, you need to move the hand in a clockwise motion a few times to put emphasis on the please word.

These are some of the basic greeting and common words that you need to hold a polite conversation with a person. From greeting someone to signing goodbye, there are many gestures that you will be using every day.

Chapter 2- Navigating Daily Life in ASL

Your routine in your daily life needs the signing of certain words and expression. Depending on what is included in your daily routine every day and at what time, you can sign different things. The things that you do daily can be signed using ASL. There are some common words and actions that we all do every day, like brushing your teeth, taking a bath, eating food. Signing for these activities can help you navigate your daily life. So, knowing and practicing these signs is important.

Every morning

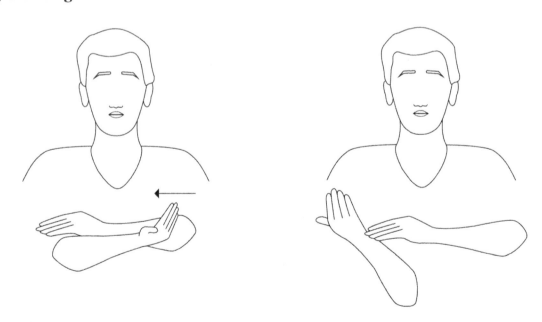

You sign the word morning by placing the left hand in a parallel manner to the floor with the palm facing down and the forearm in front of your chest or stomach level. The right hand should move and slightly be bent at the elbow as the right palm faces up and is slightly raised. The fingers of the left hand should touch the forearm of the right hand. When this movement is done in a sweeping movement, it shows every morning.

Every afternoon

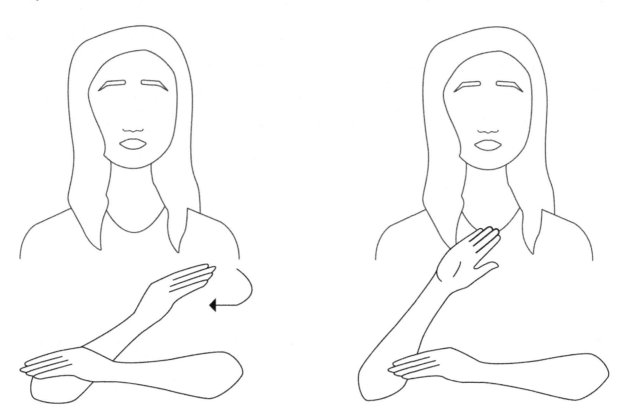

You can sign the word every afternoon to show a routine work that you do every afternoon. For example, you can do this by holding the right arm over the crook of the left elbow and then slide the sign of afternoon towards the right until it is at a single position. Only the right arm will move in this position. For the afternoon sign, you need to place your dominant flat hand at a position to show 2 o clock so that it is pointing ahead and up.

Every night

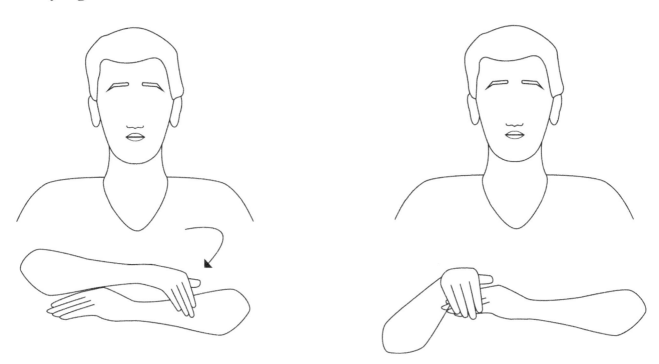

To show the sign for night, you need to place your left forearm in a horizontal flat position. The palm should be facing down. After this, you need to put your right hand's wrist on the back of the left hand and the right fingertips should be slightly bent to point down. This should be done in a sweeping motion to show the expression every night.

Early

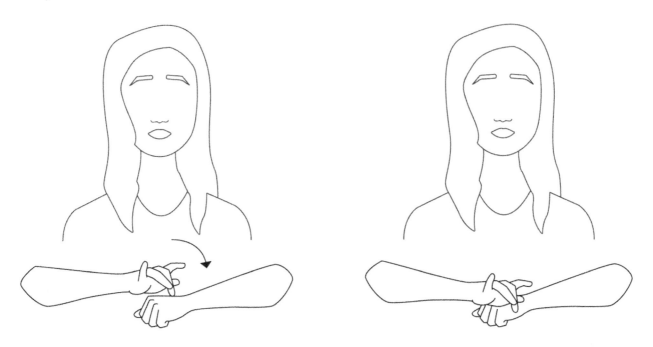

The sign for early is used to show when something is done early or If you like to wake up early etc. the sign for early is easy to make. The two hands are in the same gesture in this sign. The right hand slides over the left hand to show the sign of early or ahead of time. The left hand can be in the shape of a fist or a flat hand in this case.

Late

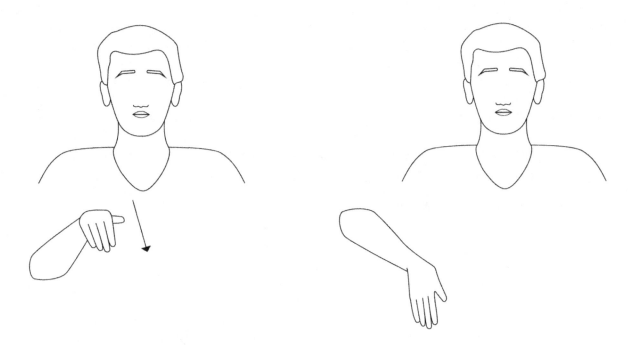

To make the sign of late, you need to raise your right hand slightly and then bend the arm in a manner that the hand is facing downward with the fingers pointing towards the floor. Then you flap the hand back once or twice to show that the time and event is being pushed back and it is late.

Now let us talk about some basic routine actions like setting an alarm, going to bed etc.

Setting an alarm

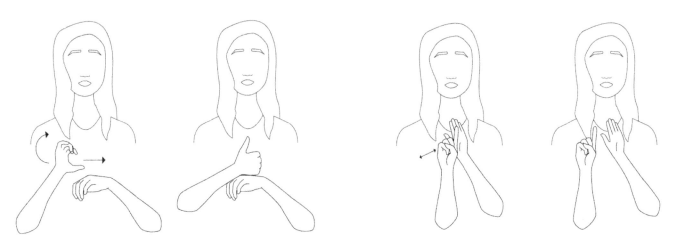

For this, you need to sign for the clock and then for set or setting up. You can show the clock or time for alarm by hooking the fingers of your right hand and then tapping it on the upper surface of the left hand. The left hand on which the watch is should be flat, horizontal and the palm should be facing downward. Once you have tapped the upper hand, your right hand then transforms into a thumbs up that is placed on top of the left hand to show the word set.

Go to bed

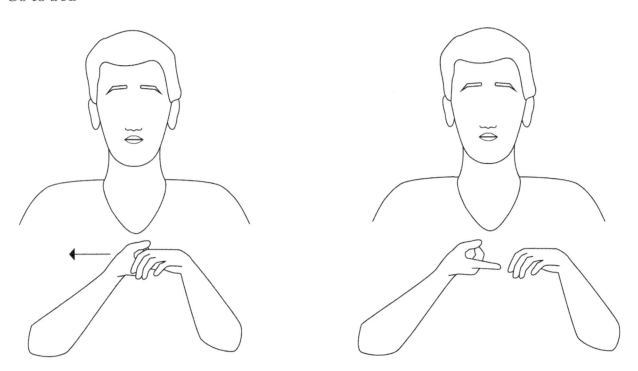

If you wish to sign, go to bed to indicate your usual routine, you can just sign the gestures for Go Bed. This can be done by putting your left hand in a resting and curved position like a C. After this, you need to bring out the index and middle fingers of the right hand and then move it towards the gap of the C made in the left hand. You can do this once or twice to put emphasis on the action of going to bed.

Wake up

The sign for wake up is a simple sign that shows the action of opening up eyes to wake up for the day. To do this, you need to close your both hands with your index finger and thumb touching each other to make the shape of an eye. Place the both hands just below the eyes, resting above your cheeks. Your eyes should be closed at this time to show that you are sleeping. Then you open up your fingers to make a L shape on both hands. When you open up your hands, you also open your eyes to show waking up.

Rest

The word rest can be used to show the action of relaxing too. For example, rest and relax can be shown with the help of flat hands and arms crossing each other, laying across your chest and shoulders to show a resting position. When you cross your arms on your chest, make sure you are closing your eyes in a relaxed manner to suggest the idea of rest.

Get ready

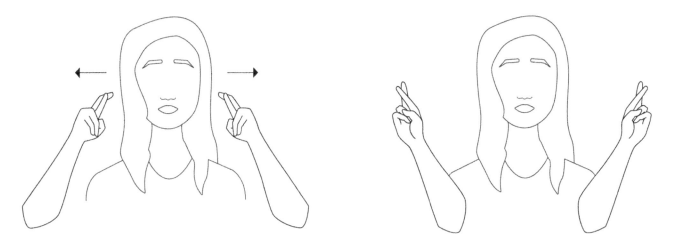

Get ready is an expression that we use to show getting ready for the day or for an event. To show the sign for get ready, you need to cross your index and middle fingers on both the hands and then bring them up to both sides facing outwards. Then you need to shake your arms so that the two crossed signs shake too.

Eat breakfast

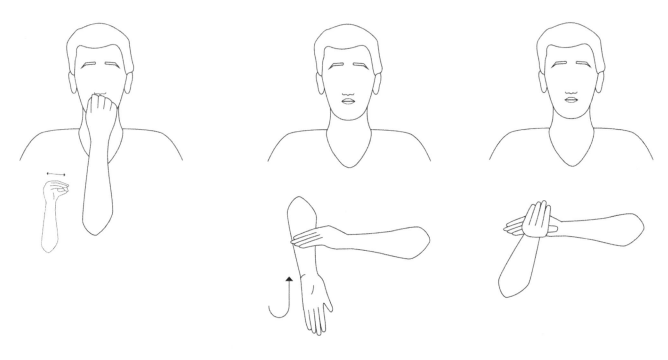

To show the sign of eating breakfast, you combine the sign of eating and morning. Eat Morning shows that you are eating your morning meal that is the breakfast. To show eat sign, you make a fist with all your fingers pointed upwards and your fingertips scrunched together to show a handful of food. Then you take this handful to your mouth and follow the sign of morning after this. You can also do the sign for eat and the sign of morning in whichever order you want to show eat breakfast. The same thing can be done with the sign of night and afternoon to show eating lunch or dinner.

Take a bath

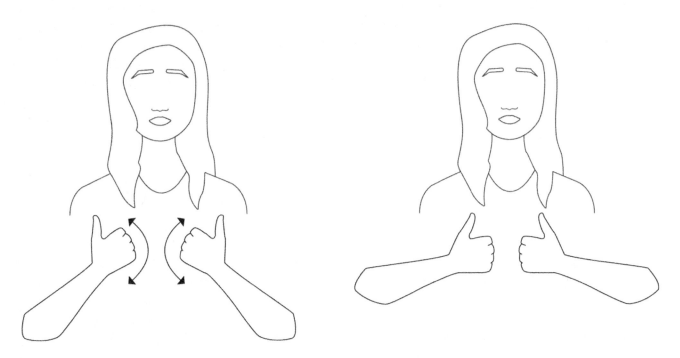

To show the movement for take a bath, you need to fist your hands with your thumb pointing out and then you need to put the two fists at chest level with the thumbs pointing upwards. After this, you need to move the two fists up and down to show a scrubbing motion to show taking a bath or getting cleaned.

These are some of the daily actions that you can describe with the help of ASL.

Chapter 3 Discussing Family and Relationships in ASL

When you wish to talk in ASL, you will also want to address your family and friends with the help of the signs. When holding signs for ASL conversations, we need to also establish the relationship between different people. Addressing family and creating relationships when talking in ASL is important for the meaning and continuity of conversations.

There are some family members and familial relationships that can be expressed using the ASL signs.

Family

Let us first start with family. You can sign the word family by signing F with both hands. After this, both your hand should be horizontally near your torso and these should be forming a circle. The two hands should be in a F sign and then the index and thumb fingers should touch each other. Then the two hands should circle each other and the pinkie should touch each other. This makes it look like you are encircling a group of people and showing that they are family.

Friend

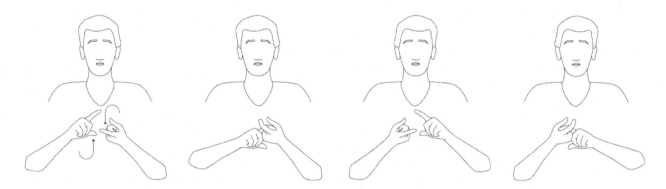

The sign friend is used a lot in general conversations. To make the sign for friend, you need to make your hand in a curved manner with the index finger hooked. One hand should be held up with your hooked index finger facing up. Then, you need to hook the second index into the first index. Then you need to reverse the position of the two and repeat the movement. This shows the sign for two friends hugging.

Father

To show the sign related with father or any other word that shows the general word for father or dad, you need to spread your hand out in a fiver and then you need to tap the thumb end to the forehead. It is also helpful to remember that male relationships and family members are generally signed by placing the signing hand above your nose. The female signs are made by placing the hand below the chin.

Mother

Spread the fingers of the right hand so that it looks like a five. Then place the hand on your chin in such a way that the thumb is touching the chin and the pinkie is facing away from the chin.

Brother

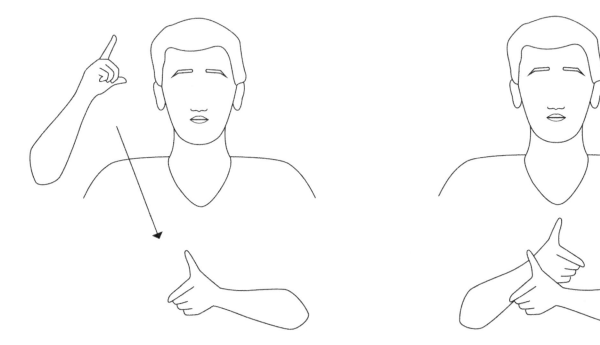

To sign the word brother, you need to shape the two hands in the shape of L with your index and your thumb extended. The left L hand should be by your chest or torso pointing outwards. The right L hand should be on your forehead with the thumb touching the forehead. Form it like you are holding to a baseball hat. Then bring it down to rest on your left hand as a double L.

Sister

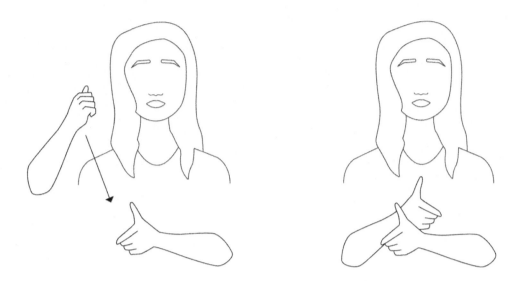

You need to do the same L shapes like you did in brother. Then you need to place the left one near your torso and the right hand should tap on your chin with the thumb. Then you need to bring the right L on top of the left L hand and tap it.

To sign all these roles in in law manner, you need to first sign the person's role and then sign the word law with your hand. To sign the word for half brother or half sister, you need to first sign the gesture for half and then you need to sign for brother or sister.

Son

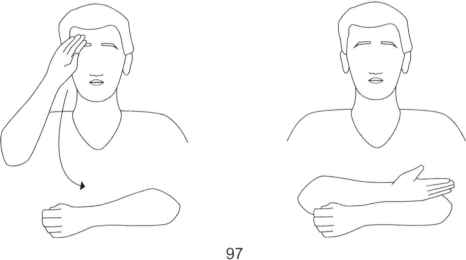

97

To sign for son, you need to sign male, and then the sign for baby. For male, you need to touch your forehead with the index finger of your right hand. Then you need to bring down your right hand and change the hand from pointing to flat hand. You then make the sign for baby by crossing your arms in a resting position. The right hand should be on top of your left hand with the hands facing up.

Daughter

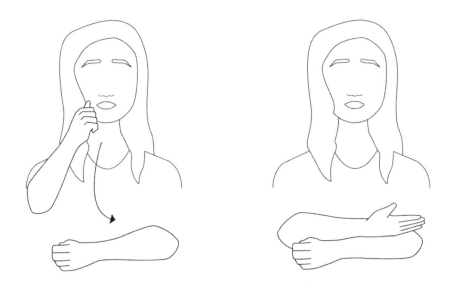

To make the sign for daughter, first touch your chin with the index tip of your right hand. Then bring the right hand down and bring it down on the left hand in a flat manner so that it forms a cradle and the sign for baby. This means a female baby or a daughter.

These are the signs that a beginner must learn to talk about family and friends.

Aunt

Uncle

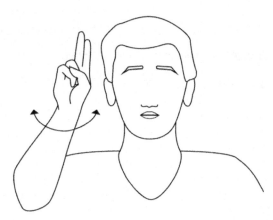

Male cousin

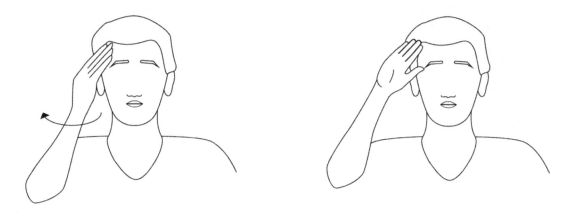

Female cousin

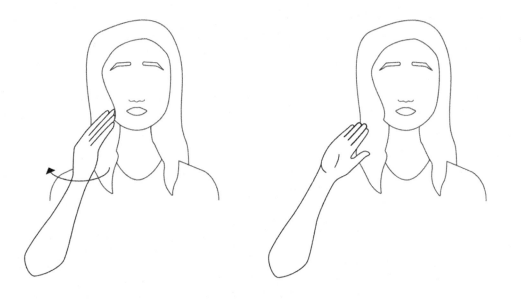

Chapter 4- ASL Vocabulary for Work and Employment

In the context of work and employment too, specially abled people need to converse in signs. There are many signs that are associated with the way words for office, work, boss etc. are signed. Signing the occupations is also an important part of talking in ASL. Knowing how to speak occupations in ASL helps you in daily life.

Work

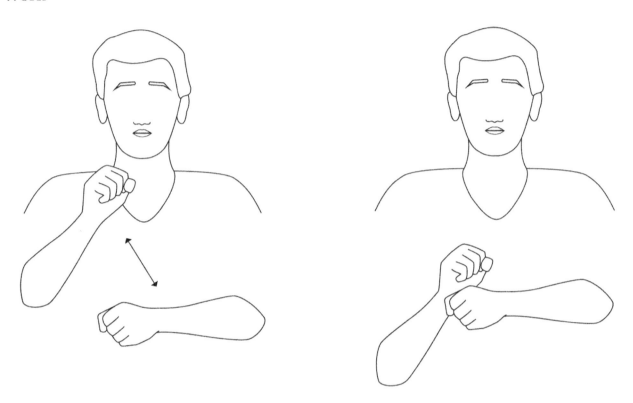

To sign for work, you need to close both the hands into fists. Then you need to tap your dominant fist on top of the non dominant fist a few times. This is mostly done in the wrist area.

Office

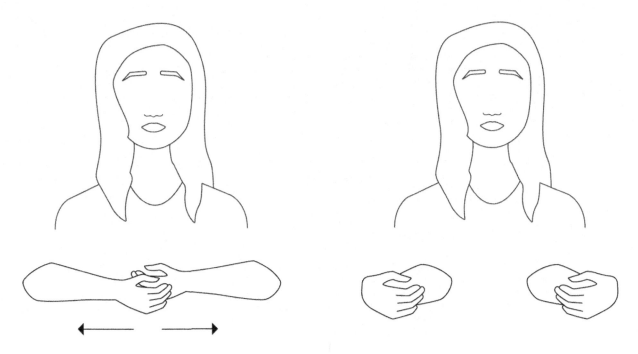

To sign for the word office, you need to form an O with both your hands. Then you need to put your forearms in such a way that the two arms are first parallel to your body and then perpendicular to your body. This makes a box which stands for your workspace.

Boss

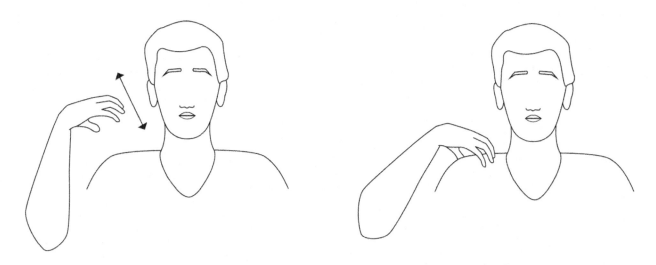

The sign for boss is pretty simple. To make the sign for boss, you need to make a clawed hand and then place it on your shoulder and tap the clawed hand twice on the shoulder. This shows that there is a lot of responsibility on the shoulder of the boss.

Manager

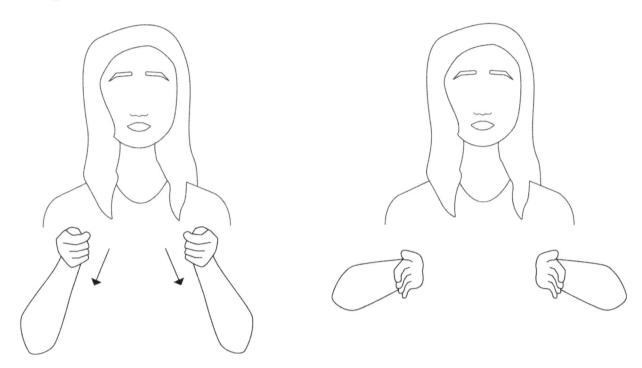

The manager is someone who manages or controls certain things. So, to make the sign for manager, you need to put your hands in a fist in front of your chest with your index finger crooked out like you are holding the reins of a horse. The hands should alternate forward and backward to show the act of control and management.

Secretary

For the role of secretary, you need to hook your right hand in a manner that the index finger is slightly hooked and up. Then you need to put the hooked finger to your mouth (closed) and then bring the hooked finger towards a raised flat hand on the left. You need to drag the hooked finger along the flat hand and then separate the two and flatten both as you bring both down to the torso level to rest at parallel to each other.

Assistant

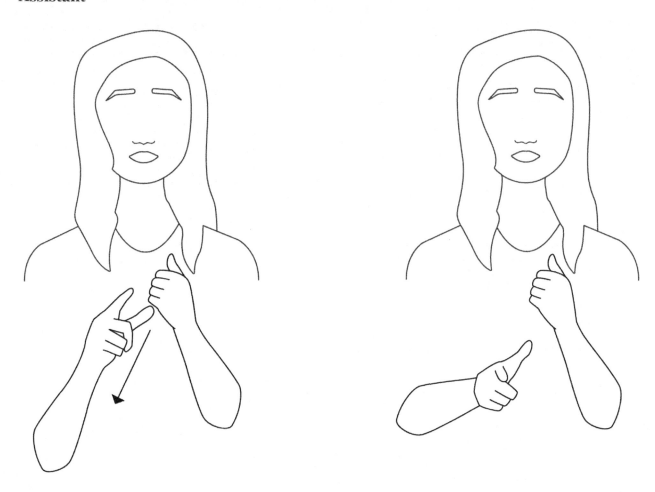

To show the sign for assistant, you need to shape your left hand like a fisted A and the right hand should be shaped like a L with index and thumb extended. The left A hand should be raised and the right L hand should be placed below the A hand with the thumb of the L touching the base of the A hand and tapping it twice.

These are some of the basic signs associated with any work space that you should know about to operate in the professional field. These signs are done in a manner that they show the different roles people have in an office space.

Chapter 5- ASL Vocabulary for Education and Learning

When in school or an educational institution, specially abled people need to communicate about their education. Gaining education is a very important goal and to do this through ASL, people need to know about the different signs associated with school, education and learning. There are many signs like teacher, student, read, write, learn etc that a person should know to show learning activities.

School

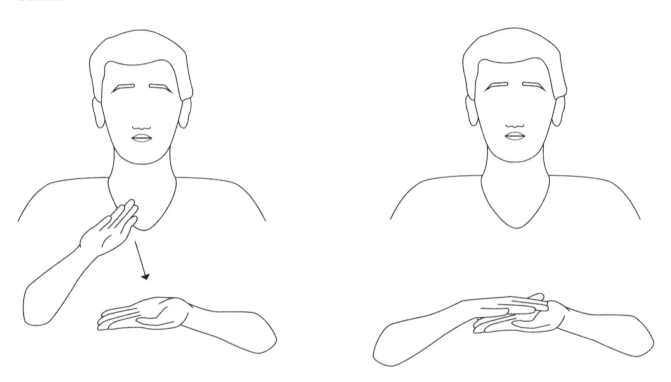

To sign the word school, you need to place both hands flat. The left hand should be flat and outward near your torso. The top hand's fingers should be aligned in a perpendicular manner with the bottom hand and then it should come down in the same angle to clap down.

Student

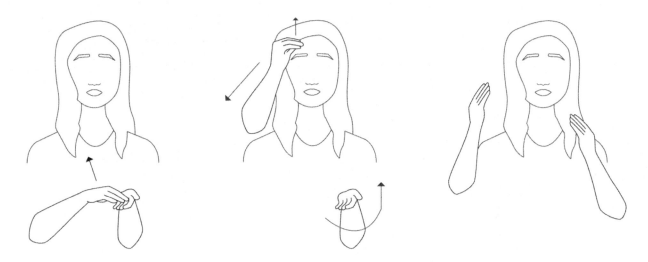

To sign student, you need to hold out your left hand in a flat manner, where the palm is facing upward. With the help of the right hand, grab some imaginary thing like grabbing information from the left hand. Lift this information and stick this to your head. This shows the gesture of learning information which is a task for a student.

Teacher

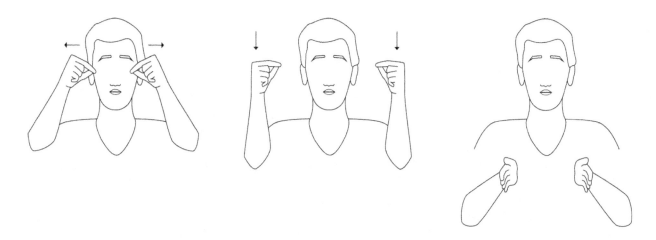

The sign for teacher is made by closing your fingers and your thumbs a short distance from the forehead. This should be done with the hands placed by the side of your head with the arms by your ears. After this, you need to open your hands so that the hands face each other in a parallel way. After this, bring the two hands down from shoulder level to waist level.

Principal

You should make the P sign with your right hand. Then you need to make the left hand into a fist or a palm face down so that the top of the hand is exposed. After this, you need to circle the P over he left hand and then bring the right hand down on the left hand.

Class

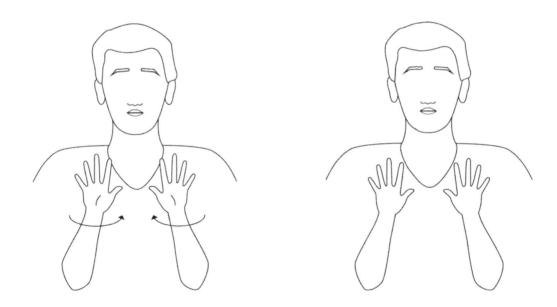

To sign for class, you need to make the hands in an open manner and then make them face each other in C signs. You need to make your index fingers and thumbs touch each other and then circle them out. This should look like making a circular plate in the air. Then you need to touch the pinkies of the hand.

College

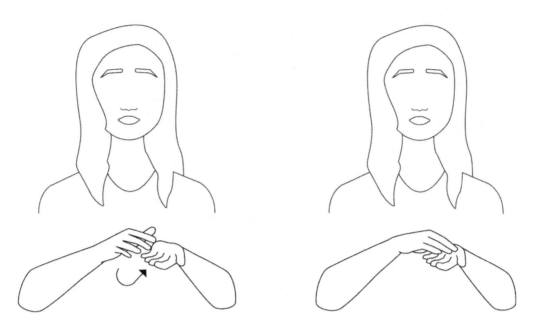

For both the college and the university, you need to place your hands in a flat manner. The right hand is placed a couple of inches above the left hand and there is a circling movement. After circling, you can make the hand come down on the left hand and slap it and then bring it back up.

Help

Suppose you are asking for help from the teacher, you would need to sign for help. To sign for help, you need to make a fist with your thumb out with your right hand. Then you need to place the right hand on the flat up of the left hand. Then you need to move both the hands in an upward direction.

Book

To make the sign for book, you need to put your palms together and then keeping your pinkies together, you need to open up your hands to show the opening of a book to read.

Learn

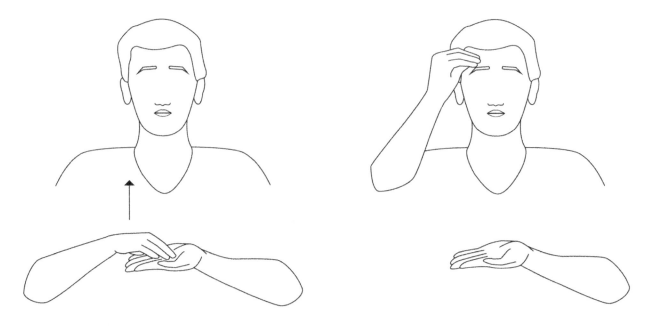

To make the sign for learn, you need to first make a flat palm facing up with your left hand. Then you need to grab information or an imaginary thing from the left palm with the right palm and take the hand to the forehead. It should look like you are stuffing information into your head into your head with the right hand

Write

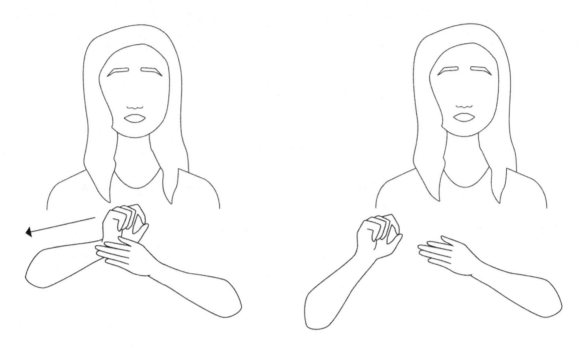

The action for write is like using a pen on a paper. For this, you need to flat the palm of your left hand. Then you need to bring the index and thumb finger of your right hand to show that you are holding a pen. Once you make that, then drag it on the open and upward flat left palm to show the action of writing.

Read

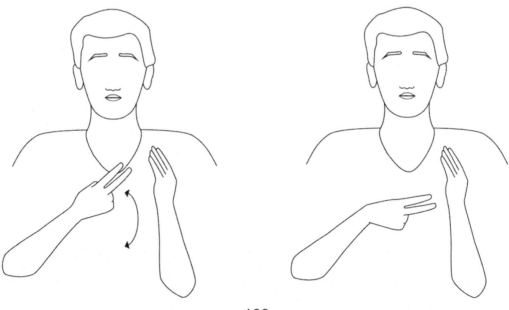

To make the sign for to read, you need to flatten your left hand and hold it up so that it faces you. After this, take your right hand and form it like a V. Then point the V towards the open palm and move it up and down like you are reading a page.

These are the basic signs that you need to learn in the school and education context. The basic actions and people involved in the process of education can be signed in this manner.

Chapter 6- ASL Vocabulary for Socializing and Leisure Activities

Most of the conversations we hold are done during socialization. As we socialize with people, we start talking and then we use ASL. So, we need to learn about the signs of ASL that are associated with social interactions and leisure activities. Below are some of the basic signs for leisure activities and social actions.

Fun

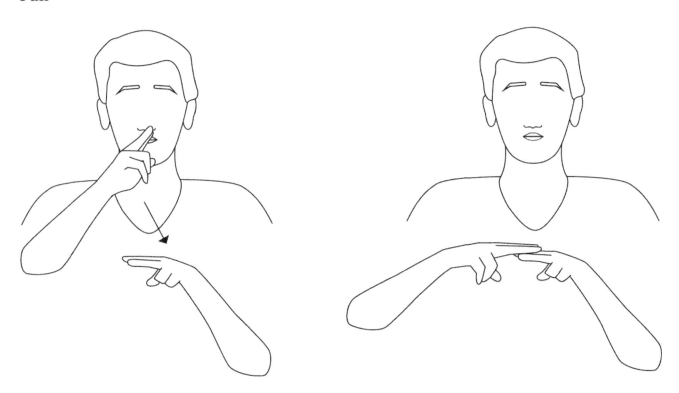

To sign for fun, you need to make both hands into fists and then extend the index and middle fingers of the right hand. Do the same thing with the left hand. However, the left hand should be placed horizontally near the torso. Your right hand starts at your nose and turns up and out. After this, you need to bring the right hand down so that it meets the left hand. You should have a fun and smiling expression when signing for this.

Party

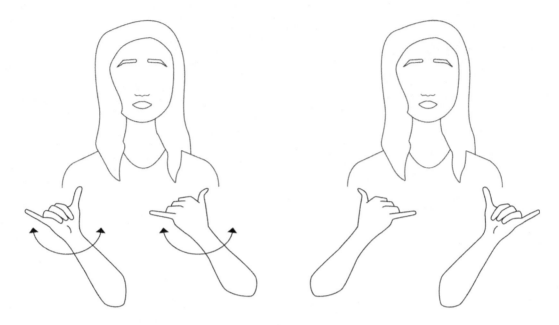

To make the sign for a party, you need to fist both your hands and then extend the pinkie and thumb of both the hands. Then move your hands in a random dancing movement in front of your body to show people having fun at a party.

Play

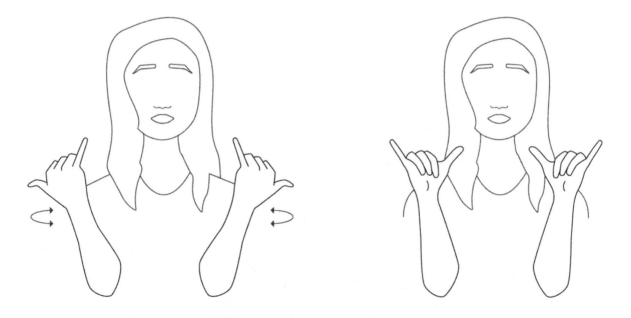

To make the sign for play, you need to make the y sign with both your hands the way you made it above. Then you need to wiggle and move the hand in front to show that children are playing with each other.

Dance

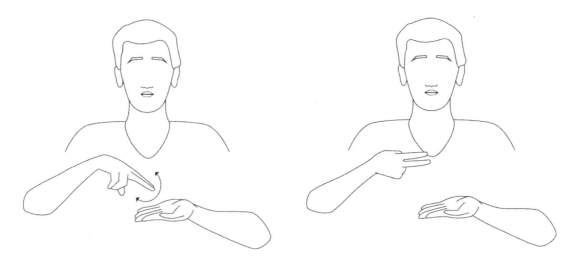

To make the sign for dance, you need to make the V sign with your right hand. The middle and index finger should be apart and straight. Then you need to extend your left hand like an open palm. Place the right hand on the open palm so that the two fingers are also propped up on the left hand. Then swing the two fingers back and forth to show a dancing motion.

Movies

To make the sign for a movie, you need to show that a person is moving on screen. For this, you need to extend your left hand in a manner that the left forearm is in front of your body and with your palm facing your body. Your right hand then goes behind your left hand and then the palm shakes back ward and forward to show movement.

Picnic

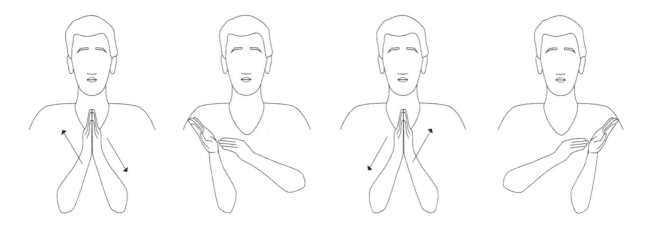

To sign for picnic, you will need both hands flat and in front of your torso. Then take your flat, open arms and face then towards each other. Then you need to brush the two palms with each other from side to side.

Trip or holiday

To sign for a holiday, you need to open both hands. The two palms should be facing each other. Then you need to rest both the hands with the thumbs near your chest. These should be at your arm pit level and then you make a tucking action. The tucking action should be such that the person looks like he is not doing any work and simply relaxing. Then you need to move your hand forward and backward.

These are some common signs for leisure and relaxation that you can use in the social context. You can use them with your family and friends or to explain a social situation.

REFERENCES

https://www.nidcd.nih.gov/health/american-sign-language#:~:text=American%20Sign%20Language%20(ASL)%20is,of%20the%20hands%20and%20face.

https://www.britannica.com/topic/American-Sign-Language

https://mn.gov/deaf-hard-of-hearing/learning-center/trainings/?id=1121-400825

https://takelessons.com/blog/asl-for-beginners

https://www.udemy.com/course/cwamerican-sign-language-introduction/

https://www.udemy.com/course/asl-with-jp/?utm_source=adwords&utm_medium=udemyads&utm_campaign=LongTail_la.EN_cc.INDIA&utm_content=deal4584&utm_term=_._ag_118445032537_._ad_657560774297_._kw__._de_c_._dm__._pl__._ti_dsa-1212271230479_._li_9153340_._pd__._&matchtype=&gclid=CjwKCAjw67ajBhAVEiwA2g_jEFFkZLDpto8IWob7YS8rL4Dtyf7QPeZObqRrBewCkljTpYqbHhjBJRoCGf4QAvD_BwE

https://frdat.niagara.edu/assets/Disability-Handouts/ASL-alphabet.pdf

https://www.researchgate.net/figure/The-26-letters-and-10-digits-of-American-Sign-Language-ASL_fig1_328396430

https://www.splashlearn.com/blog/the-abcs-of-asl-alphabets-know-the-american-sign-language/

Made in the USA
Las Vegas, NV
15 October 2023

79122356R00063